TGV INSPIRING LIVES

VOLUME 2

CONVERSATIONS THAT MATTER

NAVEEN SAMALA

PARUL GUPTA

Made with ♥ on the Notion Press Platform
www.notionpress.com

To my unwavering pillars of support—my family and friends—who patiently stood by me throughout this journey, offering encouragement and understanding.

To the incredible TGV speakers, whose wisdom and insights have enriched these pages.

A heartfelt thank you to my co-author Parul Gupta, the dedicated audience, community, well-wishers, and the universe at large for contributing to the completion of this book on time.

Your collective energy and positivity have fuelled this endeavour.

With deep gratitude,
Naveen Samala

To the Trailblazers, Visionaries, and Game-Changers,

This book is dedicated to those who refuse to accept the ordinary, who choose to embrace the extraordinary, and who understand the power of transformation. To the TGV speakers who have graced stages and ignited minds with their words, you are the architects of inspiration.

To those who believe that ideas have the potential to reshape the world, this book is a celebration of your passion, courage, and unyielding commitment to making a difference. Your voices resonate beyond the confines of a room, reaching hearts, sparking change, and leaving an indelible mark on human experience.

This book is a heartfelt thank you to the TGV speakers who have shared their insights, wisdom, and inspiration, reminding us that, indeed, the best is yet to come.

With Gratitude
Parul Gupta

Foreword

Shakti Sagar
Independent Strategic Advisor

In the past three years, I've closely witnessed '**The Guiding Voice**' (TGV) evolve under Naveen Samala's leadership. From a rising podcast to the milestone of its 400th episode, TGV has become a premier platform fuelled by unique focus and unwavering passion to make a difference.

Now, contributing a foreword for '**TGV Inspiring Lives Volume 2**' is an honour. This curated collection features over 23 diverse leaders, from Sound Healers to Visionary Leaders, each sharing profound insights from their journeys. These stories, encompassing peaks and valleys, offer transformative perspectives on breaking stereotypes and fostering personal and professional growth.

These narratives act as a guiding blueprint for navigating life's crossroads, emphasizing themes of opportunity, persistence, risk-taking, and the crucial roles of family, passion, confidence, failures, and success.

As I delved into the draft, certain thoughts shared by the contributors lingered with me:

"Life is not easy; it's about how easy you make it."
"Reconnect to Your Soul."
"Mantra for life: JUST BE."
"Pioneers may not be Entrepreneurs."
"Waiting for the perfect moment is futile; true transformation begins in the present."
"An Unbreakable Spirit of Resilience."
"Consistency, fresh ideas, and updated content. Don't focus on monetizing your content; focus on sharing knowledge and adding value."
"Find the courage to take that first step and trust yourself to figure things out as you keep walking."
"Values—devotion, dedication, determination, and courtesy—stand as pillars."

These profound insights collectively embody an unyielding spirit of resilience and provide a compass for those navigating their paths. '**TGV Inspiring Lives Volume 2**' encapsulates not only the diverse experiences of its contributors but also serves as a source of enrichment for readers seeking profound insights into the human experience.

In the spirit of the contributors' shared wisdom, I encourage readers to embrace positivity, cultivate calmness, and find contentment in their journeys. **Be Positive, Be Calm, Be Content.**

Shakti Sagar

Preface

Welcome to the second volume of '**TGV Inspiring Lives**'. As we pen down these words, we are filled with an overwhelming sense of gratitude and excitement. The journey that began with the first volume has been a remarkable exploration of the transformative power of ideas and the inspiring voices that propel us forward.

With **TGV Inspiring Lives Volume 2**, we delve even deeper into the realms of inspiration, guided by the belief that stories, insights, and wisdom have the potential to spark change and illuminate the paths less travelled. 23 Speakers with their unique stories - this book is a celebration of the relentless pursuit of excellence, the courage to embrace growth, and the unwavering vision that propels individuals to make a lasting impact on the world.

As you embark on this journey through the pages that follow, we ask you to open your mind and heart to the diverse voices that grace these narratives. Allow the wisdom shared within these pages to be a compass, guiding you through the complexities of life and inspiring you to reach for new horizons. From the bustling streets of urban landscapes to the serene beauty of rural roots, each narrative is a celebration of the human spirit.

Thank you for joining us on this odyssey of inspiration. May '**TGV Inspiring Lives Volume 2**' be a source of motivation, reflection, and, above all, a catalyst for positive change.

*We are on a mission to shape the careers and lives
of millions across the globe.*

Prologue

From Dream to Reality: The Unlikely Journey of The Guiding Voice Podcast

The Journey of a thousand miles begins with the first step.

Origin of The Guiding Voice (TGV):
In the early days of the pandemic, March/April 2020 marked the birth of a daring vision. Fuelled by newfound insights from a transformative Podcast Mastery course with Bijay Gautam, the idea of podcast ignited within Naveen Samala. He wanted to run a podcast- a vessel for stories and insights. Until he was just an avid listener of podcasts and never imagined starting one by himself

Yet the journey commenced with a call to a friend who, for reasons unknown, missed the initial invitation. The fate played its part, nudging him to dial a second number—Venkata Sudhakar Nagandla (His partner during the initial years of the Podcast journey). In that call, the foundation of the venture was laid. The Guiding Voice in English emerged as their inaugural creation.

However, it's essential to acknowledge that **Faceless Voice** was a joint initiative with Venkata Sudhakar Nagandla in 2019, a project that they couldn't sustain beyond 15 episodes of pep talk due to time constraints. Despite this initial setback, the vision endured, evolving into a more resilient form in the wake of the pandemic.

The initial spark ignited a desire to expand their reach, to share interviews not just through audio but with the visual allure of YouTube. However, the sheer magnitude of the undertaking gave them a pause. The path to launching interviews on this expansive platform seemed daunting.

As the world ushered in 2021, a year of growth beckoned. The interim period became a learning ground—a classroom for mastering the intricacies of video editing. It was a skill set acquired, a tool added to his creative arsenal, laying the groundwork for the unfolding chapters of his podcasting journey.

In the relentless pursuit of knowledge and adaptation, the narrative began to take shape. What started as a simple decision boomed into **The Guiding Voice** platform. It is not just a podcast anymore but a testament to the uncharted territories explored during a time when the world yearned for connection and storytelling.
Therefore, the seeds of ambition were planted, anticipating their transformation into a set of diverse voices and stories.

The ink of Inspiration: The Guiding Voice Inspiring Lives (series of books)
Amidst the podcasting endeavours, the spark for the 'TGV Inspiring Lives' series was kindled in the aftermath of our milestone 100th episode with Prof. Jagdish Seth on The Guiding Voice (English). It was a moment that stirred the imagination—a moment when **Vidyadhar Prabhudesai** extended an intriguing proposition. 'Why not publish a book encapsulating the nuances of 100+ conversations?' he suggested.

The idea, though intriguing, loomed with uncertainty. The leap into the realm of publishing felt like uncharted terrain. Yet, the universe had its way of nudging Naveen forward. A mysterious international courier arrived from Scott J Miller (CMO of Franklin Covey Leadership Institute and the host of the '**On Leadership**' podcast). Upon unwrapping, he discovered it was a signed copy of Scott's book '**Master Mentors Volume 1**'. The book about 30 prominent guests that Scott Interviewed, their stories became a source of inspiration for Naveen.

The resonance was undeniable. Inspired by the richness of Scott's work, a decision solidified—to birth a series of books featuring the voices that echoed through **The Guiding Voice**. With Sudhakar Nagandla as his companion in this literary voyage, they faced a daunting reality—they were novice writers. The solution materialized in the form of a collaboration with seasoned authors.

Naseha Sameen, a name that emerged as a potential collaborator, didn't merely jump into the project; she leapt with enthusiasm. From that point forward, there was no looking back. Naseha's authorial expertise became the guiding compass, steering them through conversations about their target audience, the number of featured guests, and the practicality of book sales.

In the chapters that unfolded during those discussions, the ink of inspiration flowed freely. The series began to take shape, a testament to the synergy of diverse voices converging on the pages of the **TGV Inspiring Lives** books. It was a journey of exploration, learning, and the alchemy of turning spoken wisdom into the written word.

With the immense success of **TGV Inspiring Lives Volume 1**, Naveen decided to launch Volume 2 in 2023 along with Parul Gupta. And the plans are already on to launch Volume 3 and Volume 4. This is another effort to share the stories of unsung heroes with the world.

Embracing the Canvas of Failure

In our lives, we often showcase the vibrant threads of our successes, proudly narrating tales of accomplishments. But how often do we dwell upon the chapters of failure? Did we ever consider finding out what our favourite failure is?

Broadly, we encounter two distinct categories of failures in our lives: avoidable and productive failures. The former, draped in emotions of shame and embarrassment, are the outcomes that perhaps could have been averted with better planning or research. The latter, however, are the missteps that, in hindsight, appear as steppingstones to unforeseen successes.

Consider your favourite failure. Is it the one that led you to something unexpected, something larger and more profound?

Is it intertwined with the failure that imparted the most valuable lessons?

Such favourites often emerge from what we term "productive failures"—errors that, when reflected upon, reveal invaluable lessons and pave the way for future successes.

Reflecting on Naveen's journey, a particular failure stands out—the non-selection for a premier leadership program (Corporate Audit Staff) during his tenure with GE. The disappointment lingered, contrary to his expectations and the leaders around him.

Yet, this failure birthed a cascade of opportunities. It paved the way for roles as a corporate mentor at JAGSOM B-School in Bengaluru (formerly known as IFIM B school) and a guest faculty at BITS Pilani WILP division. These opportunities facilitated connections across India and propelled him into the role of Operations Program Manager at GE in 2015.

This failure became a mantra—he started telling himself that failure is not final, nor is it fatal. It is merely a nudge to keep going, to keep striving. The post-failure period became a canvas for analysis, a time to acknowledge the domino effects and lessons it unfurled.

David Ward aptly notes, ***"Failures reveal weaknesses, errors in judgement, and areas needing improvement"*** Embracing this mindset, we dissolve the negative connotations attached to failures. As we mute the pessimistic views, we find ourselves liberated to try new things, share ideas, and ardently pursue our desires.

A challenge to the reader is to reflect on your failures, not with judgment, but with appreciation. Share and cherish them, for they are the crucibles of your growth. As you pause to reflect on your favourite failure, consider sharing it on social media. Tag **Naveen Samala**, **Parul Gupta** and **The Guiding Voice**, using the hashtags *#tgvinpiringlivesvolume2* and *#tgvilfavoritefailure*.

In this exploration of failures, remember—they are not stumbling blocks but stepping stones, guiding you toward a more enlightened and self-aware version of yourself.

How to read this book?
This book stands independently of **TGV Inspiring Lives Volume 1**. It offers a fresh narrative and perspective. You may read the chapters in any order. Re-read and reflect on the stories to learn from both the successes and failures encountered by each of the speakers featured in this volume.

Table of Contents

1

Cathy Nesbitt: The Worm Advocate and Ecopreneur who is Harnessing the Power of Laughter

Did you know worm composting is possible within the confines of your home?

What hits you when you first hear the word vermicompost?
For us, it is a lot of organic waste, soil and a big ground to dump it all under to let the magic happen.

If you have seen it at your home or have done the gardening by yourself, you would be familiar with the idea of vermicompost. We add it to our plants once every few days to maintain the plant's health. It works just as vitamins and other supplements work for your body. Since the food can't give all the nutrients, you consume supplements to overcome the deficiency. And while Soil is essential for binding, composting is the best manure for your plants. Much more interesting is the process of making it.

The organic matter/kitchen waste when decomposed in the soil is consumed by Earthworms. They give out a part of the matter as excreta, also known as vermicasting (vermicompost). The vermicast contains nutrients that work as rich manure for plants. This improves soil structure by increasing the water and nutrient-holding capacity of the soil, leading to providing more nutrients to plants and enhancing their growth hormones.

To summarise, it is a process wherein you decompose organic waste and the worms in the soil digest this organic matter to transform it into beneficial soil. Good quality compost is temperature-controlled and can be accomplished in a shorter time.

We used to have a fair idea of composting. To be honest, we got half of the concept right. Till our co-author and podcast host, Naveen Samala met and recorded this podcast with Cathy Nesbitt. And then we discovered that creating vermicompost is as easy as a walk in your park. All you need is some soil and a smile on your face while the waste decomposes, and you get the vermicompost. The best part of talking to Cathy was not just this business she was running but her infectious laughter. Later we got to know that besides working so close to nature, she also is a laughter yoga instructor. Our co-author, Naveen Samala, himself is into laughter yoga. So now you can listen to the podcast too for some interesting conversation on Laughter Yoga while you also learn a few techniques.

Talking of Cathy's journey into such a niche business, this was not her first instinct. Cathy was in Toronto, Canada and making ends meet with her 20 years of a corporate job. But a part of her always felt heartbroken because of the climate crisis around us. When she witnessed how Canada started exporting garbage to the USA, a part of her wanted to do something so she could give back to nature something better than just a dump. It was when she came across the term 'vermicompost' and eventually read more about it to enhance her knowledge of the subject.

For her, **Knowledge is power.**

She didn't want to leave this knowledge as another piece of information stored in the brain. Cathy acted upon it and decided to be an entrepreneur in the field. She established her brand, Cathy's Crawly Composters, in 2002 and there is no looking back since then. She didn't just focus on selling the compost but also educating the masses about it and creating awareness of how beneficial it is for nature. To spread the message, she left no stone unturned! From getting hosted on podcasts to seminars, she did it all. She created awareness of keeping the kitchen waste and creating compost instead of dumping a pile of garbage for Mother Nature.

It is pretty safe to say, or how Cathy labels herself, **A worm advocate.** The phrase grabbed Naveen's attention and got her to The Guiding Voice.

Her awareness programs took her to many places and events. It is in one of these events that she happens to meet a potential client who is also a preacher of Laughter Yoga. She got fascinated talking to him and once again her life motto, "Knowledge is Power" made her curious to learn more about it. She began her journey of acquiring knowledge on Laughter Yoga and practising it as well.

'Laughter Yoga' was initiated in India in 1995 by Dr. Madanlal Kataria. It is a stress-busting breathing exercise that aims to bring joy and abolish physical and spiritual ailments. What started as a way to deal with stressful situations became a part of a club in Mumbai where the individuals started practising it daily. And as they say, *Laughter is Contagious!* This form of yoga spread worldwide and now has 5,000+ clubs spreading the message of Laughter Yoga with daily practice. As simple as it looks, Dr. Kataria claims that laughter yoga helps strengthen your immune system and increase energy levels. This eventually helps the body fight a lot of chronic diseases and promotes overall positivity of thoughts. No wonder, this initiative of Dr Kataria got worldwide recognition and in one of the columns, the London Times titled him as a '***Guru of Giggling***'.

Practising Laughter Yoga helped Cathy at all levels. Be it dealing with her hardships or the stress of entrepreneurship. She became a regular in the Laughter Club in Toronto and witnessed health benefits herself. What started as a curiosity, soon turned into becoming a passion for her. From being a trainee, she is now a certified trainer of Laughter Yoga. Dr. Kataria himself appointed her as a worldwide Laughter Yoga ambassador in 2017. So out of sheer curiosity, we decided to ask Cathy about her version of Laughter Yoga. And her take on this is as simple as explaining the difference between a joke and laughter.

"Jokes are not for everyone, it is cultural. But Laughter is a universal language. When you laugh, the brain stimulus gets triggered into letting go of your ego and letting the facial muscles work to reflect more of yourself. A burst of stimulated laughter in Laughter Yoga tricks your brain into understanding it as natural laughter".

Not only that, Laughing also triggers all your LOVE drugs (DOSE)-
Dopamine
Oxytocin
Serotonin
Endorphins

It is pretty safe to say now, *We Love this Drug **DOSE!***

At present, Cathy Nesbitt is running a successful vermicompost business while also being a Laughter Yoga instructor to help people deal with all the stress around them. She lives on the mantra of **gaining as much knowledge and putting it into action**. She loves to travel and has already covered 30 countries in 13 months of travel, starting as young as 27. And we can't give her curiosity and love for life any less credit for shaping her into the woman she is today.

We are glad to know about her passion towards saving Mother Earth and we hope readers will do their bit towards it. You can connect with Cathy in case you need any support.

Our rapid-fire round with Cathy was as interesting as talking to her about Laughter Yoga, full of fun!

What is your favourite failure?
My very first vending event was an eco-fair in 2002 when I started my worm business. Being in an environmental event, I targeted selling a lot of worm composters. My husband and I prepared for three weeks making sure we had enough material for the bins, including shredding paper, sifting soil, drilling holes in the bins and much more. Although there was a lot of foot traffic and attendees at our booth, we did not sell anything for two days! Near the end of the second day as the event was winding down my in-laws arrived. My Mom-in-law felt so bad that we didn't sell anything, she bought a worm bin to support us. Our only sale of the day. This event was a wonderful lesson in business for us.

What are the hardships you went through while going through your life/career journey?
One of the challenges I faced with Cathy's Crawly Composters and the worm business was the lack of public awareness. Although composting is nature's way of looking after our organic matter, the idea of worms in the house was not a familiar concept back in 2002. People don't buy what they need, they buy what they want and not everyone wants worms in the house. I pivoted to doing worm workshops and speaking in the media to raise awareness about the benefit of using worms to convert food scraps and paper into nature's finest fertilizer.

What was the planned vs actual career path for you?
When I was growing up, the only options I knew for working women were secretary, nurse, stewardess, waitress, and teacher. I thought it was a limited list and chose the secretarial path. I took all the office worker courses: short hand, typing, etc. I was a great secretary but got bored easily and changed jobs every year.

The universe is a fascinating place. In 2002, the landfill for the Greater Toronto Area (Canada) closed and we started to export our garbage to the United States. Almost 1000 trucks weekly! 6 million people live in Toronto. Half live in condos, townhouses and other places without space for outdoor composting. I had a solution for one of the world's biggest problems: organic garbage. One thing led to another, and Cathy's Crawly Composters was born. As an entrepreneur, my business has ebbed and flowed adding products and services along the way to create a wider offering. My working title is Cathy Crawly Laughing Bean Queen. Simple solutions for today's challenges. Worms for amending the soil, sprouts for eating and laughter for overall health and wellness.

What was the turning point in your life?
The 1980s was my decade of travel. Three months in Europe with my then-boyfriend, now husband. I lived in France as an *au pair* for a year to learn French. Spent nine weeks travelling across Canada, then 13 months in Africa and Asia. Travel shaped the woman I have become.

One person that influenced you the most & how?
Not one but there have been many influences over my life. My stepfather, Mike, played a pivotal role in how I live my life today. My parents separated when I was 7 years old. Mike moved in with us when we left the family house. He lived with us for 14 years. I loved him so much. He was gentle, wise and a great listener. We had a wonderful 'father-daughter' relationship. When I went to live in France, Mike said to me, "It's not going to be the same when you return." When I returned, Mike had brain cancer and died shortly after at age 38. I feel like somehow, he knew. Mike's death made me realize that life is short, and we never know. I vowed to never stay in a job that didn't serve me, and I never did.

One incident that transformed your life.
In 1993 I moved from an apartment in Toronto to a small town and I bought a house. I was excited to start composting and gardening. A Teacher friend asked me to look after her worm bin for the summer. I knew the value of the worm poop for gardening but didn't want

worms in my house. I like to try new things so I took on the challenge. It didn't work out like I thought it would, but I did manage to keep the worms alive. In 2000, I graduated with a psychology degree after 15 years of night school (1985 - 2000) and got a job at a group home working with dual-diagnosed adults. They had 10 homes and a farm but didn't compost. When I mentioned composting, the greenhouse manager said, "What about worms?" That was when I knew an awareness of compost and worms was much needed.

What is your Vision/Goal/ in life and What are you trying to achieve?
Right from the start of my business, my goal was to put worm composting in every living space, every home, every classroom, and every business. With worm composting happening onsite, we no longer must truck this organic resource around.
My other goal is to spread the DOSE (Dopamine, Oxytocin, Serotonin, and Endorphins) as a Laughter Yoga instructor and incorporate tapping, brain gym and other healing modalities to help people get out of stress and into joy.

What is one hidden fact about you?
I am a certified graphologist (handwriting analysis). My husband and I became certified upon returning from our 13-month trip. We had a business, The Write Impression, doing handwriting analysis. It's interesting what can be learned from writing. As handwriting was a dying art, we transitioned onto other ventures.

A favourite fantasy gadget that you want for yourself/want to invent.
A Magic carpet – it exists in the movies. Imagine silently flying around without emitting greenhouse gases.

If you are not at work, what do you like doing?
I enjoy walks in the forest, spending time in nature, camping and cycling. Gardening and learning new information and of course laughing for the health of it.

How do you keep yourself up to date? Please share links or references to websites/blogs/books etc.
I follow '**Untethered Soul**' by Michael Singer

One piece of advice you want to give to the youngsters in the field.
Be sure to schedule time for yourself. When running a business, it can become your life so make sure you LOVE it. If you do not enjoy it, over time you will hate it. When you are stuck, get out in nature. Step outside. Go for a walk. This will clear your head and make space for the answers you were seeking.

What are your thoughts about The Guiding Voice platform?
The Guiding Voice is inspiring and informative. Learning from entrepreneurs around the world is inspiring and helps everyone do better. The platform works a charm for sharing experiences and knowledge for a sustainable future.

Tune into Cathy's episode here:

2

Preeta Pradhan: A Sound Healer who is a synonym for Re-Invention

Is it possible to heal through the magical power of Sound and Energy?

If you have read Malcolm Gladwell's **Tipping Point**, you would be instantly able to connect when I say the word **'connector'**. If you haven't, Malcolm Gladwell, the author of The Tipping Point, defined in his book that a connector is someone who knows an impressive number of people in a community, more than an average person knows.

Recording many podcast episodes with individuals and getting in contact with more people through them made me a connector too. But if I have to count on one of the major connectors from my life, it is my dear friend Kavita Garla. She introduced me to many wonderful souls, including Preeta Pradhan. Her introduction to Preeta started with a phone call about how a warrior in life Preeta is and is now a certified sound healer. If you know me, this is one fact that I get inspired by individuals who fought through the odds of negatives and made it happen for themselves and the community.

Preeta's journey against breaking societal norms started when she graduated to become a computer programmer in 1985. An era where being a female in India and achieving a professional engineering degree was rare. Under the circumstances, she mastered working as a programmer on an 8/16-bit machine. While you are working on 32-bit and 64-bit today if you are curious about finding how an 8-bit machine would work for complex programming, look for the microcontrollers and systems on a chip.

After her marriage, along with her husband, she had to move to Assam and leave her job because the technology was so nascent at that stage that remote work was not an option. In fact, people never thought there was a possibility of remote work as we have today.

Not every day it happens that you are prepared for what life has to throw at you. But when we talk about Preeta, we talk about a woman with perseverance and resilience. She found the best in the situation and decided to pursue a B.Ed., as teaching was the only option for her. Soon after, she got a job as a teacher at a local school in Assam. She feels proud that she worked as a teacher for a good 10 years of her life and thoroughly enjoyed her profession.

But life had more to teach her!

So, after switching between two entirely different career paths, life threw another challenge at her on the personal front. She had to leave her 22 years of unsuccessful marriage along with her kid. And it wasn't an easy decision to make! Belonging to Indian society, divorce for a woman comes with a lot of challenges from the community. It was a tough walk but taking a stand and working her way out is all that Preeta knows.

Or as she puts it, "*I just lifted myself out of a dark place*".

To suffer is a choice, and she chose not to.

The roller coaster of life made her re-discover herself every single day. After living through the tough process of divorce, her only focus was on healing herself. She took the path of transforming for the better. Worked on herself for 3 years and after each day of self-discovery, she decided to give her all into sound healing. It started with her joining a gong bath** session for 3-days. A not-so-comfortable session when you are going through emotional turmoil, but everything you need at the moment; making you meet your suppressed emotions. Using sound as a form of healing dates back to ancient cultures. Sound healing sessions are considered when you want to relax or heal your emotional body or bring your mind, body & spirit to an equanimous state. It brings up hidden emotions which remain in your emotional body. Sound healing works on the energy body. Every cell in our body vibrates at a certain frequency, our complete body could be understood as an orchestra of all the different parts of the body vibrating at different frequencies. As we grow in life, each & every body part holds some impressions, and memories which may lead to some of the parts getting out of tune, hence re-tuning is required.

Putting it in more scientifically - Recall the Pendulum oscillation experiment we all have done in the physics lab as a kid. When pendulums oscillate and then you strike one pendulum at the end and find that all pendulums then start moving at the same pace. Sound healing works on the same principle of Cymatics*

How does it work?
It is the same as how breathing works in Yoga! You can't see it but just the right breathing uplifts your mood and has an impact on your overall mental health.

Sound Healing works on the same principle. It is all about creating the right frequency and vibration. When we are vibrating at low frequency, we feel stuck. When we vibrate at high frequency, we feel lighter and move forward easily. The frequencies generated in sound healing slow down brain waves for you to attain a deeply restorative state. And a slow brain is known to activate the body's self-healing mechanism.

From vocal chants to instrumental sound healing, all the frequencies helped Preeta to feel balanced with her emotions and replenished her thoughts. Having benefited from sound healing personally, she wanted to spread it to the community and became a healer herself.

To become a healer, first, one must get healed and start the journey of self-healing. Any healing modalities need to be practised on oneself before we start healing others. Self-healing is a way to experience the magic of understanding the different dimensions of our existence. Preeta's suffering over the years and her profound will to heal gave her the strength to walk out of what was not meant for her. She worked as a healer for the people who needed it. [1]

Her life's purpose is summarised in a mantra,
'Free the individuals from suffering by walking through it and not by ignoring it.'
At present, you will find Preeta as a nomad in the mountains! She took the bold step of leaving her house and adapting to a slow pace of living by moving to the

---

[1] **Gong baths are a type of inactive meditation, where you "bathe" (getting immersed) in the healing vibrations of sound.
*Cymatics' is the science of visualizing audio frequencies.

mountains. At the time we interviewed her, she was in Rishikesh, leading a minimalist life in uncertainty and yet feeling content because of the inner peace she attained over the last few years. We are curious about what her next destination would be!

And since we never end the conversation on a serious note, here's an interesting rapid-fire we had with Preeta:

What has been your childhood fantasy picture?
I wanted to be a horse rider.

What's your favourite book?
Black beauty! Well, it is about a horse.

Can you describe yourself in just one word.
Resilient

What is one thing that you would change in your past?
Wish I had known about self-love a little earlier in life.

What is one electronic gadget that you'd like to see or invent yourself?
Not invent but I would love to own a gadget that measures the energy of an individual daily, the thermometer for energy measurement.

If all this makes you curious about sound healing or you want to make a career in it, connect with Preeta. You will find her LinkedIn profile URL & QR Code in the **speakers'** section.

> **Question to Self:**
> Wherever I am in life right now is because I want to be there. Or is my security becoming my bondage?

Tune into Preeta's episode here:

3

Joshua Shea: Breaking the chains of Addiction.

From Porn Addiction to Empowerment: A Captivating Journey of Transformation

"Porn addiction" - Did we just make the room uncomfortable for you by mentioning this 'word'?

We sure did! After all, we are living in a world where stigma and shame often shroud discussions about sexuality and addiction. And open conversations remain a rarity. Individuals grappling with porn addiction find themselves entangled in a web of embarrassment and judgement, causing them to retreat from seeking help and opening up about their struggles. Cultural taboos further complicate matters, with conservative attitudes towards sex stifling the ability to openly address the issue. The lack of awareness about the legitimacy of porn addiction aggravates the problem, as many perceive pornography as harmless entertainment rather than a potential addiction.

On top of it, even media coverage doesn't always alleviate these barriers; it can, at times, sensationalize stories or focus solely on extremes, preventing a balanced discourse on the matter. But never about the porn addiction of individuals. A part of it concerns the privacy of individuals, discouraging them from sharing their experiences openly. But if anything, the lack of education and resources dedicated to addressing the risks and signs of porn addiction compounds the issue, resulting in fewer conversations about the topic.

But as always, we at **The Guiding Voice** are there to take the unconventional path to approach society. And reached out to Joshua. From a promising journalist and creative film festival creator to a respected local politician, Joshua seemed to have it all. However, beneath the surface, he battled a tormenting secret—a pornography addiction that spanned 24 agonizing years.

And before you form a judgement here (or not), let us spill some facts -
The ubiquity of pornography is unsettling; Pornhub alone received 42 billion visits in 2019, surpassing combined visits to Netflix, Amazon, and Twitter. This raises a pertinent question: is porn addictive? While the scientific community debates its classification as a medical addiction, Joshua Shea's journey offers a stark glimpse into its destructive impact.

Joshua, an individual living in Central Maine has always been a workaholic. And his "busy schedule" did involve addiction to alcohol and porn for a good 20+ years. It was when he started down a road that it hit the critical point in the addiction cycle as he was drinking three times a day. He started looking at porn more than once a day and it made the transition from just looking at video clips passively online to going into chat rooms and talking with women. He was only sleeping two or three hours a night. So, there was this perfect storm coming together and he ended up being awake till one or two in the morning, talking to women online.

It was almost as much about power as it was about sex, that he ended up speaking to a girl who was a teenager. He found out about a year later that she was only 14 years old. One day in early 2014, the Maine State Police showed up at his door with a warrant to check his computers. He was arrested and became the headline of the newspaper the next day. The embarrassment of facing society, his wife and his family was too much for him.

But if anything, Joshua is thankful for the day he got arrested. It was the beginning of the next phase for him - confronting and recovering from the porn addiction! He dug deeper into himself and decided to talk about it. To start with, he normalized talking about this addiction for the world. He decided to write down his story in a book, as a cautionary tale for people who are living in shame and embarrassment that they're dealing with this.

Joshua, being a journalist, dug deeper into this subject. Determined and armed with newfound clarity, he interacted with other addicts and embraced self-discovery. His journey illuminated a vital truth: education and accessible resources empower recovery. Support groups, therapy, and documentaries empowered and guided him to take the path of transformation.

But recovery was a daunting path laden with uncertainty and challenges. Yet, within this struggle, the glimmer of hope was the decision to write a book on his journey. A book to channel his pain - about pornography addiction, resonating with countless others silently enduring similar struggles. Messages from fellow addicts and their partners ignited a purpose—to help others trapped in the same.

While working on the book and collecting the data from other porn addicts he recognized the societal implications of pornography's influence. He openly advocated and proposed to have an open discussion with children about the dangers of excessive porn consumption. He envisioned a future where knowledge guides the complexities of human sexuality.

We are not denying it either as facts paint a clearer picture of the issue. Between 5% to 10% of internet users may grapple with problematic sexual behaviours, possibly linked to porn addiction. Exposure to pornography starts at a surprisingly young age, around 11 years old. The impact on relationships is evident, as studies show married men using pornography are less content in their relationships. Moreover, excessive porn consumption can lead to sexual dysfunctions and risky sexual behaviours, particularly among adolescents. The brain's response to porn can mirror that of substance addiction, highlighting the seriousness of the issue.

Joshua's book - *The Addiction Nobody Will Talk About* compels readers to initiate change, confront their demons, and embrace healing. It's an invitation to self-discovery, resilience, and growth—a testament to overcoming challenges and finding empowerment. From Addiction to Empowerment resonates as a story of triumph, urging readers to seek support and embrace transformation.

Through this captivating narrative, readers understand the complexities of addiction and the power of empathy. Joshua's journey catalyses introspection, encouraging readers to confront challenges holding them back from a fulfilling life.

Joshua's journey illustrates that education, understanding, and the courage to share stories can facilitate recovery. As readers turn each page of his book, they uncover the profound impact of one man's quest, igniting a movement that empowers lives worldwide.

As fun and thrilling it was to have Joshua talk about Porn Addiction, much funnier is this rapid-fire round we had with him.

What is your favourite failure?
Building a film festival out of nothing that had a successful four-year run. Unfortunately, my addictions came calling and my partners bailed because I was no longer dependable, but those few years we ran the festival were wonderful.

Share some hardships you went through while going through your life/career journey.
I didn't finish college, yet I worked in industries that usually demanded a degree. No matter how good I was at being a newspaper reporter in a small town or being a publisher of a magazine for a large region, I have always bumped my head against a glass ceiling put in place by people who think those without a college degree cannot, and should not, attain certain levels professionally. My addictions were always a challenge in life. Hiding them from friends, family, co-workers and bosses was not fun. Whether it was alcohol or pornography, I always felt like I was living a different, secret life. Keeping track of my lies got to be challenging.

What was your planned career path and where did you finally end up?
I knew that I always wanted to be a writer of some sort, but I thought I'd spend most of my career in Hollywood writing movies. I never imagined I'd be a journalist. And then if that weren't enough, after I got into recovery I became a speaker and author about pornography addiction and during the pandemic I took up coaching. Now I coach people with pornography addiction and betrayal trauma. I would have never believed I'd be this kind of one-on-one helper in the past.

What is the major turning point in your life so far?
When I was voted out of a job by the other people who owned the publishing company with me because I was showing up for work intoxicated and making poor business decisions. Being fired was my rock bottom and I sought treatment shortly thereafter. I've been in recovery ever since and I feel like a new person.

What is one incident that transformed your life?
The birth of my son. 20 years later, he's one of my best friends in the world and I couldn't imagine having travelled the path of life over the last two decades without him being a constant.

What is one thing you would do differently in the past?
I would go back to being 3 or 4 years old and somehow communicate to my parents that the woman they thought was a good babysitter for me was a traumatizing monster. If I could have avoided the abuse that took place in her house against me and other

children, I'm curious how different a person I would be today.

What is your Vision/Goal/ in life and what are you trying to achieve?
Professionally, I want to keep going down two tracks. First, I'd like to continue working as a one-on-one coach. I get the most fulfilment out of that. Second, I'd like to continue my public mission of educating people about pornography addiction.

What is the Craziest/Naughtiest thing you have done in childhood?
There was more than one time, after a night of blackout drinking between the ages of 15-18 that I would wake up in a strange place and have to figure out where I was and how I was going to get home. Unfortunately, this continued well into my 20s.

What is one favourite fantasy gadget that you want for yourself/want to invent?
It's cliched, but a time machine. We get so little time on this Earth. It was here and everything was fine before you existed and once you die, it will still be here and everything will still be fine. I'd like to see what those times are like.

What is one piece of advice you want to give to the youngsters in the field?
It's not the smartest people or the hardest workers who win in life, it's those who are the most adaptable to the situation.

What are your thoughts about The Guiding Voice platform?
I think it's wonderful that you're able to provide a diverse group of guests the opportunity to spread education to so many people across the world. Education is the key to all of the world's problems, and you're taking it on, one guest at a time.

Quote or Anecdote that you strongly believe in?
Turn your pain into purpose.

Question to Self:
Am I being completely honest to myself and facing my addictions? Am I willing to make changes for a long-term positive impact?

Tune into Joshua's Episode here:

4

Avrum Geurin Weiss: a Psychologist's Journey from Therapy Sessions to Bookshelves

What if there is a guide to understanding Men and improving relationships with them?

You heard me right! I am talking about men and their emotions!! And if you are wondering what about it? or, What's the deal here? As they usually don't care and barely have any intense emotions!

Well, I am about to prove you wrong. Or say, our speaker and Psychologist, Avrum Weiss, is about to prove you wrong, with much-needed evidence!

If you have read **Men Are from Mars and Women Are from Venus**, a self-help book written by American author and relationship counsellor John Gray, you would be aware of the central thesis of the book. The core idea of the book is that men and women are fundamentally different and have different needs, desires, and communication styles. And that means, they feel different emotions too.

Avrum Weiss has been a therapist and a teacher of therapists for over 50 years. He has been counselling individuals and couples for over three decades now and that leads him to some really interesting findings. And many of these revelations you will find in his book, **Men's Fears of Women**. The book came into being because over the past decade, Avrum, as a psychologist, started working with men more extensively in therapy and he felt the need for the masses to resolve the underlying issue with men's emotions.

On working more with men, he realised that they are afraid of women and their surroundings. As women are more expressive emotionally, men feel overwhelmed by the intensity of it. Not only this, most of the men talked about their unhappiness in their relationships but were also not willing to talk and resolve it with their partners. *Wondering why?* For one simple reason! They didn't want to come out as vulnerable and weak in front of their partners by confronting their emotions; validly so, because we have been conditioned that men don't cry.

What makes men afraid to confront their emotions in front of their partners?
To put it in one word, it is conditioning! Men are instilled with the trait of being independent –emotionally. They are taught to be the tough ones and hence perceive it as keeping their guards high so that no one can reach them. In the process, they get detached from understanding their own emotional needs too. When a woman walks into their life, they feel afraid to be dependent on them for their emotional needs and hence avoid being expressive. All of it makes them hyper-independent, taking care of and doing everything by themselves. And this has nothing to do with how supportive the woman in their life is or how well she understands them. It is more of their thought that men are meant to be hyper-self-reliant and not ask anything from anyone.

Well, at some point in time, we all have overheard a lot of men in their 20's and 30s saying," We don't need a woman." They see the need to have a partner as a sign of weakness. And fears of getting dominated and controlled. They don't feel self-sufficient with the thought of living to their partner's expectations - financially, emotionally, and sexually.

All these findings and the need to address men across the world led to Avrum's book, ***Men's Fear of Women***. As much as the title makes you pick up the book, the journey leading to authoring this thought-provoking book is equally interesting. When Avrum was 19, and in college, he started working as a night manager in a residential treatment program with teenage addicts. His job was to stay at the centre at night. On one sweet night, he had a dream about one of his faculty. The faculty died without publishing his work of a lifetime. Though just a dream, something made Avrum reach out to this faculty and share this with him. And before he knew it, they both started working on the book. It took them just 7 years to author their first book. As amazing and as bizarre as this sounds, we are now hoping a lot of you to remember your night dreams and make the relevant ones a reality!

What played a key role in Avrum's journey of writing is - Opportunity, Persistence and willingness to take risks. All because he is passionate about what he does!

So why are Men Afraid of Women?
One simple reason - Men fear co-dependence!

A relationship with an opposite gender comes with co-dependency and being vulnerable - allowing another person in your space. But men are conditioned to not ask for help and hence they act like they don't need women.

But counter to it, as Avrum says, ***"Men get into a relationship faster than a woman does after every breakup."***

And that explains Men need to seek a partner but do not admit it consciously.

If you are smiling reading this, you know what we are talking about! ****wink****

Since we managed to put a smile on your face, let's take you to a psychologist's instincts with this Rapid Fire to make you smile wider

Tell us a lesser-known fact about you.
I can juggle two balls and an apple and eat the apple while juggling.

What is your favourite childhood fantasy?
To be a writer and I did it after 40 years!

What is the best advice you have received so far?
My Dad quit his job in mid-life and went to change his career at a much less salary, but it was his passion. The best advice I got from him was - Don't sit around and wait for things to happen, make it happen.

What is one word that describes you the best?
Listener (We can't agree more!).

What is your favourite failure?
Close to 35 publishers rejected my book.

What is one piece of advice you have for The Guiding Voice audience?
Do not prioritise money in your life. Follow your passion and work hard for it instead of just wishing for it.

2 years ago, Avrum left his home of 43 years and moved to an island on the main coast. He enjoys all the outdoor activities - Boating, hiking, kayaking, gardening and woodworking.

While this was one of the most fun podcasts we have recorded, more interesting was the learning about human behaviour in relationships! We recommend you read Avrum's book with your other male friends. And discuss your underlying fears with them. When you are truly ready, confident and comfortable with your emotions and feel having them is just being a normal human, go talk to your female counterpart.

An emotion expressed in the right way never goes unaddressed.

Question to Self:
Do I know and understand my emotional fears? If not, what am I doing about it? If yes, am I able to express it to my partner?

Tune into Avrum's episode here:

5

Mary Alice Arthur: Building Bridges with Storytelling

Have you ever met an activist who is uniting people through the common language of storytelling?

Coming from a place of recording podcasts and writing the second edition of this book, we totally vouch for the power of conversation. And how each conversation counts as a story of the individual in itself.

Stories have the power to shape our worldviews, inspire us, bring us together, and create change. This is also the foundation of the work of a story activist, someone who uses storytelling as a tool for social change. Story activists are passionate about creating an equitable, and compassionate world, and they believe that stories can help us get there. Whether through writing, speaking, facilitating, or simply sharing stories, story activists are making a profound impact on communities around the world.

Mary Alice Arthur is one such renowned storyteller, activist and TEDx speaker. We got a chance to host her on our Podcast on the recommendation of a good friend, Pankaj Mishra. And the positivity Mary got with her was prodigious. She has dedicated her life to using storytelling as a tool to inspire change and bring about social justice. She has travelled around the world, sharing her stories and encouraging others to share theirs, in order to create a more empathetic and understanding world.

As offbeat as this profession may sound to you, Mary's journey to becoming a storyteller, started in childhood. She learned to walk in 10 months and by the age of two years, she was opening and closing the doors. Way ahead on the growth curve!! Well, that should have been received as a fair warning for her parents that she understands things quickly. She used to read two books simultaneously while going to school and loved everything that she could get her hands on. Little did she or anyone around know that a story activist was in the making!

It took her 30 long years and presence in an International Storytelling festival in New Zealand, *The Glistening Waters**, to realise the power of storytelling and its impact on the world. It is at the festival that she happened to meet a New Zealand-based Hollywood actor - Cliff Curtis.

In his speech, he said, *"People who tell stories are activists because a good story makes you want to do something. A good story hits your hand and the head at the same time and then it makes your hands do something. It makes you do something."*

To validate this, Mary's friend jumped in with the response that,

"The most important Real Estate is between your ears. And you decide who is going to live rent-free here"

Did she need more validation for the skill she has been carrying since childhood? We guess, not!

And so we got our Mary Alice Arthur - The Story Telling Activist. In her terms, a Story activist is someone working with stories for a positive systemic shift and using critical intelligence on pertinent issues. Simply put,

"I create spaces where the right story can take people to the next life-giving future that they're longing for."

Interestingly, her first experience as a storyteller activist was not on a public platform but in a car. She was on a drive with her mother when she narrated the story of losing her loved ones early in childhood, for the *nth* time! It is then when Mary told her mom to change the narration from being a victim to shaping into the strong lady she has become because of her childhood incidents. Her mother took it positively and Mary got her confidence to tell people that they are the anchor of their own thoughts. This was her first experience motivating someone to use a story as an experience to retrospect and grow.

Forward to 2003, the term "organizational storytelling" came into being. At the same time, Mary's house of 7 years was sold. Credit to her positive attitude she counted it as an opportunity to do something different with her life. She packed her stuff and became a nomad, travelling with all her stuff in the back of her car. And finally now coming down to just one suitcase and travelling with her storytelling skill. Over the years, she became a great listener and learned how to trust. That only helped her become a name in storytelling.

Her work as a storyteller activist has taken her to all corners of the globe. She has worked with organizations like **SOAR** (Significant Orientations, Amazing Results). SOAR helps leaders in organisations, collectives and communities be the visionaries, changemakers and new paradigm activists they want to be, through supporting them and their people to find, craft and live a clear, compelling story that creates a powerful presence and leads to a more flourishing future. She has facilitated workshops, led storytelling retreats, and spoken at conferences and events, all with the goal of using storytelling to bring about social change.

One of the most notable projects that Mary Alice Arthur has been involved with is the Story Dojo. This is a community of practitioners who use storytelling to create more sustainable, collaborative, and resilient communities. Mary Alice has been a key player in this community, using her storytelling skills to help others tell their stories and build stronger, more connected communities. She is also the author of the book - 365 Alive, Find Your Voice, and Claim Your Story.

Mary's impact on the world is not limited to just being a storyteller. She talks about listening as much as narrating the story. *As she puts it,*
"Listening is love in action. And no storytelling can happen without listening."

She never fails to give credit to her listeners. And her work has inspired countless people to share their own stories and use them as a tool for change. By helping people connect through their stories, she has created a ripple effect of empathy and understanding that has had a profound impact on communities around the world.

Mary's passion for storytelling is contagious. And we are pretty sure this chapter must have left you inspired to share your own story with the world in some form or the other. The internet is all yours, and so are we!

Reach out to us and let's record a podcast on your story. We would love to do that! Not only that, but you never know, your story might be part of our future volumes :)

We know you are waiting for the Rapid-Fire round with Mary because it definitely was fun for us to have a rapid round of Q&A with a storyteller.

Would you travel to the past or future?
Well, I'm a Geminian, so I would have to say both. You know, people in the past have asked me: would you like cream or yoghurt, and I would usually say yes to both, so I think it would be both.

I have a sense, I don't know my deep sense is it's all gonna work out, you know like we could learn to love each other, so I'd like to go to the future and see if my idea is right – and there are some people in the past, I think would be wonderful to catch up with some of the great storytellers of all time, wouldn't it be wonderful to sit at their feet for a moment and hear them.

What is one random skill that you would like to learn?
That is interesting. I have a lot of colleagues who are graphic facilitators, their ability to draw something and capture the story in their drawings is magnificent. I like doodling with my coloured pencils and things like that, but I think I would If I could learn how to do that kind of

thing because I think stories and images have been human capacity for a long time.

What is the funniest moment in your life so far?
Back in the 90s, I was in Zimbabwe, and the border was very strict. On a random day, I decided to cross the border, just to get another stamp on my passport. I ended up in a place between countries. I was near a river called the Zambezi, what Zimbabweans call the "smoke that thunders" because of the falls. It was amazing, but instead of staying there, I walked further into the neighbouring country, leaving all my money behind.

As I was regretting my decision to leave a scenic place, I turned back and heard someone calling me. I started walking faster, and two guys approached me, one carrying a giraffe carving taller than me. They asked if I could help them get the carvings across the border so they could make some money.
I was hesitant, thinking it sounded like smuggling, but I agreed as long as I didn't have to touch anything. We crossed the border, I helped traffic a giraffe carving, and once over, we went our separate ways.

Looking back, it's a funny story, but at the time, I couldn't believe I was involved in such a strange situation!

One favourite fantasy gadget that you want for yourself/want to invent.
The moment I read of Hermione Granger's beaded bag with the Undetectable Extension Charm on it, I wanted one! Oh, the luxury of having everything you need

without having to carry it with you! I spent many years as an intentional nomad living out of my suitcase with no fixed address. Living like that makes you very focused on having only exactly what you need and nothing more AND it makes you realise that the word "luggage" has "lug" at its core. Mostly I travelled with a suitcase of around 25 kilos -- it is my weightlifting training! To flit around with a small, beaded bag still set up a whole base camp. Wow!

What was the turning point in your life?
I've had a few turning points. I was an exchange student at the University of Hamburg when I met someone who was an AIESEC trainee. AIESEC was at that time the largest student organisation on the planet and offered traineeship for students to work in businesses around the world. A chapter started at my university, and I joined it. I worked for the national office in New York City and then for the international office in Brussels. From there I went on a traineeship to New Zealand working for Ogilvy & Mather Advertising and stayed for almost 30 years.

One person that influenced you the most and how?
Back in 2007, I read Christina Baldwin's book STORYCATCHER. In it, I read about a practice called "The Art of Hosting" and about one of its founders, Toke Paludan Møller. That year I happened to be on a team organising a facilitator's conference in Edinburgh and we invited him to open it with me. To this day I'm not sure why he said yes. He didn't know about the meeting, and he didn't know me. But I've learned that Toke can sense where he's needed. He would say: "I can smell it." Since that time, we've been practitioner

mates, working and learning together and I am now also a steward of the Art of Hosting community (http://www.artofhosting.org), working and teaching around the world. How he practises participatory leadership and hosting conversations that matter has profoundly influenced my view of how these processes work, what it takes to bring together people who've never collaborated before and to shape them into highly effective and respectful self-organising teams. I've watched both him and me deepen into leadership. And, what I love most about working together is cracking a new pattern and being in joyful learning together. It's a gift to have someone like this at my back, inviting me to be my best.

What are your thoughts about The Guiding Voice platform?
I love the variety of topics this podcast takes on there's always something intriguing to stimulate questions and provoke new viewpoints. Where else could you learn about storytelling, sex, design, content creation, personal transformation and leadership all in one place?

Question to Self:
How can my story create change or bring awareness to a particular issue? What are some potential next steps I want to take for further engaging with storytelling as a tool for activism?

Tune into Mary-Alice's episode here:

6

Vidyadhar Prabhudesai: A visionary leader who took the road less travelled.

His legacy serves as an inspiration to us all, reminding us of the profound impact that one individual can have when driven by a vision of creating a better world.

Have you ever thought about corporate social responsibility beyond what your company participates in every year? Or have you thought of making a change but are still stuck on where to start?

This book is all about the inspirational stories of individuals next door. Those who stepped up and turned conditions favourable for them. Vidyadhar Prabhudesai is one such leader. But before we introduce you to all the feathers in his cap, let us introduce you to him first as an individual before a leader. And his story starts at an airport!

Vidyadhar started his career with a top MNC in Bengaluru. As he progressed in his career, he started getting frustrated with corporate life, even though he was working with an employee-centric company where his career growth was taken care of. So his frustration was nothing to do with the company or its work culture but with the exhaustion of not doing anything meaningful for the country. It was one fine evening when he was taking a flight back home for his Mother's birthday. Just before the take-off, he decided to step down from the flight and stay at the airport till he could take another flight in the morning.

Don't we all know the power of slowing down and doing nothing? It is in this brief moment that we realise what we want from life!

Such was this moment for Vidyadhar. And he took the bold step of quitting his job over a text at this very moment. Now he was jobless and without a plan of what to do next. He had no idea what he would get into, but he chose his inner calling over the corporate baggage he could have carried for life. He relocated back to his hometown, Mumbai, and tried to thrive on some partial income sources. But soon the embarrassment of failure swept in and with some limited savings and an educational loan he got enrolled in a management program. But instead of getting into corporate this time, he decided to address the entrepreneurial streak in him. Vidyadhar joined LeadCap, an early-stage startup as an employee, and climbed the ladder to become the co-founder.

LeadCap Ventures works with international governments and prominent institutions like The United Nations(UN), The World Bank Group, and The World Economic Forum(WEF) across 40 countries in Asia, Africa, and Europe. The organisation works under the curator of the Global Shapers Community, an initiative of the World Economic Forum. The main aim is to help people from marginal backgrounds to learn skills that can generate employment for them. They cover soft skills and computer skills. For the same, the organization makes sure to have meaningful tie-ups, both with institutions and government. Through innovative programs and partnerships, LeadCap equips individuals with the tools they need to thrive and contribute positively to society. Vidyadhar's vision for LeadCap is to break the cycle of poverty and enable individuals to reach their full potential.

LeadCap was recognised by the Indian government and other governments overseas. They soon became an integral part of international institutions working towards the upliftment of the backwards by providing necessary education and life skills.

Vidyadhar's advice to the young generation is to learn constantly and upgrade themselves as any learning becomes obsolete after 2-3 years. Also, have a mentor or coach guiding you throughout. If you want to reach out to international institutions for opportunities, keep a tab on the frequent openings in their fellowship programs, internships and developmental projects.

Vidyadhar's inspirational journey doesn't end here!

While his professional growth was all about going international and making them contribute to the upliftment of the backward class in India, his personal life was taking another roller coaster ride. He became a father to a baby girl! And as happy as it may sound to you, the road to becoming one was not easy. And if we may call it, destiny made him a father and has given us **'Adopt India'**. We know you are curious to know his story now. We won't keep you waiting!

On a random day, Vidyadhar came across a small girl in the bushes. Abandoned and bitten by insects, she was critical when he found her. He took her to the hospital. It took the kid a couple of months in the ICU to be fine again. As heartbreaking as it sounds to us, just wonder about the impact of witnessing it all by an empathetic person like Vidyadhar. He took the next best step and adopted her.

This whole incident also got him thinking about the number of kids who are abandoned by their biological parents because of several reasons. Vidyadhar Prabhudesai stood out and became a beacon of hope and an agent of change. His passion for creating positive social change led him to co-found Adopt India. Recognizing the complexities surrounding adoption in India, Vidyadhar and his team worked tirelessly to streamline the adoption process, collaborating with government authorities and child welfare organizations. Their goal was to provide a platform that connected prospective parents with children in need of loving homes, revolutionizing the adoption landscape in the country.

Through Adopt India, Vidyadhar Prabhudesai has facilitated numerous adoptions, giving countless children a chance at a brighter future. By simplifying and expediting the adoption procedures without compromising child safety, Adopt India, in a short period, became a trusted partner for prospective parents. Seeking to provide a loving and nurturing environment for children in need. They tirelessly work with corporates, encouraging them to provide maternity and paternity leave to people who have adopted. While also working with schools and colleges to provide free education for adopted kids. Not only this but through his awareness campaigns, he is trying to put relevant and bright signs on all the adoption centres so people can reach out to them in case they want to leave the child and not just abandon them anywhere.

Vidyadhar's unwavering commitment to transforming lives has garnered recognition and accolades, both, nationally and internationally.

For his efforts, Vidyadhar was awarded the 2nd Highest Civilian Award of Thane City, the World Bank Youth Prize Award and a Global Shaper by the World Economic Forum.

Vidyadhar Prabhudesai's work extends beyond the practical aspects of adoption and education. He has been a vocal advocate, conducting workshops, seminars, and awareness campaigns to challenge societal perceptions and misconceptions surrounding adoption and education for underprivileged individuals. By addressing common myths, fears, and stigmas, Vidyadhar aims to create a more inclusive and compassionate society that embraces the value of every individual, regardless of their background.

Vidyadhar Prabhudesai's journey as the co-founder of Adopt India and LeadCap Ventures demonstrates the transformative power of compassion, determination, and visionary leadership. And we are sure it must have got you thinking about the ways to contribute to the betterment of society.

But wait! Vidyadhar enjoys having fun as much as he enjoys doing social work. So, here's a fun rapid-fire round we had with him.

What is the one craziest/naughtiest thing you have done in childhood?
I used to keep a watch on people who travelled frequently for work away for 3-4 days. Whenever they were away, I used to take out petrol from their scooters and sell it to roadside stores etc and make money.

What is the one hidden/unknown/least known fact about you?
There were some exceptions in my case, where I messed it up and even got kicked out a couple of instances during the early days of my career. I was an absolute newbie stuck on the corporate ladder. My mistakes had cost these organizations a few hundred thousand dollars –the monetary losses and other collateral damages, and I soon realized I was a misfit in this type of work culture. I thought it would be better to part ways rather than cause further damage.

What is a favourite fantasy gadget that you want for yourself/want to invent?
I am not fond of gadgets but if the Time Machine is real then I want to go into my past and even into the future.

If you are not at work, what do you like doing?
Now it's all my daughter's time.

How do you keep yourself up to date? Please share links or references to websites/blogs/books etc.
I look for podcasts, and video blogs which are on economy, politics and business. There are many I refer to including the most popular ones like All Indians Matter, Akash Banerjee etc.

What are your thoughts about The Guiding Voice platform?
It talks about life beyond careers i.e., communities, whether it is LGBTQ, Sex education, Child Adoption etc.

Quote or Anecdote that you strongly believe in?
"Ups and downs in life are very important to keep us going because a straight line even in an ECG means we are not alive." ~Ratan Tata.

<table><tr><td>

Question to Self:
What legacy do I want to leave when leaving the world? With my paying capacity and resourcefulness, can I create sustainable systems that continue to make a difference?

</td></tr></table>

Tune into Vidyadhar's English Episode here:

7

The Journeyman's Journey to Self: Unveiling the Wisdom of Rob Grover & Gary Logan

Is it possible to dive into the mystical to rediscover one's highest purpose?

In the journey of personal growth, the transformative power of self-awareness emerges as a guiding light, illuminating the path to authenticity and purpose. This chapter of **TGV Inspiring Lives Volume 2** explores the profound journey of self-discovery. It is our personal favourite for the reason that it is intricate between personal accountability and the quest for genuine selfhood takes centre stage. The transformative narrative of Rob and Gary becomes evident that success, for them, is not just an external achievement but a harmonious fusion of dedication, devotion, and an unwavering focus. Their story serves as a beacon for those on a quest for deeper self-awareness, navigating the complexities of entrepreneurship, and embracing the vulnerability inherent in the pursuit of a purposeful life.

Rob Grover and Gary Logan have been transforming lives since 2018 through their venture **'The Journeymen Collective'** - a contemporary shamans based in Canada that guide people through an acceleration of the ever-evolving experience of awakening awareness to universal truths and higher purpose within the entire human collective. The Journeymen Collective co-creates deeply transcendental & sacred psychedelic plant medicine journeys by guiding you through the metaphysical wilderness of your soul so that you expand your awareness of multidimensional reality to accelerate your conscious impact in life, love and business.

For more than 40 years Gary has developed a deep awareness of the mind-body-spirit connection within human beings. His journey of self-exploration began when he embarked on his career as an actor. Gary explored many ways into the stillness of mind and body through fitness, meditation, music and dance, with a primary focus on studying the Alexander Technique with his first teacher in London, England. Throughout his life, Gary was continually learning that a deeper awareness of the psycho-physical connection would help him liberate the destructive subconscious programs from his childhood. Everything in Gary's life, from teaching the Alexander Technique to Healing Touch, culminated into a quantum leap once he embarked on his first shamanic journey to assist him through a time of grief and mild depression.

The numerous personal and spiritual paths that he has explored were all woven together into a deep and broad tapestry of true soulful expression in collaboration with Robert to form The Journeymen Collective. Gary was shown the shamanic path is his higher purpose. He is deeply committed to awakening people from their slumber to help them access the richness of the present moment on an ever-increasing frequency.

Rob Grover on the other hand, had a profound awakening in the year 2003. This opened him to the knowledge of deeper realms of existence. For the first two years, he was left with a typical Western approach that left many questions unanswered and deeply unfulfilled.

Robert's awareness was grounded in understanding reality when he discovered his first spiritual teacher. It changed the entire course of his life, leading him out of a successful corporate career that he pursued since his youth, onto an ever-evolving path of self-mastery. By following his deep inner guidance, Robert was led to his shamanic journey, where he remembered that his higher purpose is to help others connect to their innate guidance systems and universal truths through the shamanic path. He learned to honour and offer the dynamic flow of unique metaphysical technology, that is continually unfurling within him, for the people that embark on their journey.

Combining his lifelong exploration of science with mastery of his multisensory spiritual awareness allows every client to be energetically prepared for the shamanic journey. Robert's quantum energy work provides a deep cleaning and clearing so that the client can activate their greatest potential from within themselves and be a human catalyst impacting the entire collective consciousness.

In the world of Rob and Gary, success is not just a destination; it's a journey paved with dedication, devotion, and an unwavering focus. As we delve into their secrets, we uncover a narrative that goes beyond mere accomplishments, revealing the profound impact of ingrained values. ***These values—devotion, dedication, determination, and courtesy—stand as pillars, shaping the very essence of*** their triumphant story.

But success, as we learn, is not a one-dimensional tale. It's a profound exploration that takes us into the depths of personal responsibility—the cornerstone of entrepreneurship. Since Rob and Garry established themselves in such an offbeat trail, we did take the liberty to ask them about their journey to success. Through the lens of Rob and Gary, we realized that true success demands a willingness to confront oneself, embrace vulnerability, and release the need for external validation. It's a journey that transcends mere business acumen, delving into the transformative power of self-awareness and the courage required to confront the shadows within. And this journey is the onset of the toughest lesson —the realization that ultimate responsibility rests on the entrepreneur's shoulders, devoid of a safety net. It is the vulnerability of entrepreneurship, highlighting the imperative of self-discovery and the journey of illuminating one's shadows.

Gary's voyage to spirituality commenced in the realm of theatre school during the late '70s, a pivotal period that laid the foundation for self-discovery. His deep awareness of the psycho-physical connection, through the Alexander Technique- an embodiment of mind-body conscious awareness training, is a key distinction of The JourneyMen Collective work that prepares the whole being for the ceremonies and facilitates a dynamic integration process; from the spiritual to the physical embodiment of renewal. During spiritually intense work we often forget about the physical structure; as the human being releases old thoughts and emotional patterns from the quantum fabric of reality the physical structure requires support to unfurl away from the old faulty sensory awareness.

The shared vision of both these individuals was always open-ended, symbolizing a commitment to growth and exploration. And it was sheer luck that they both met each other! A shared quest for self-discovery and healing—a journey that continues to unfold with each step taken into the realms of the mind, body, and spirit.

In the realm of plant medicine retreats, Gary incorporates the Alexander Technique as a transformative methodology. This technique serves as a pivotal element in guiding participants towards a profound embodiment of the work undertaken during the retreat.

How does it work?
Individuals often find themselves disconnected from various aspects of their bodies, such as arms, legs, and limbs, as well as their thought processes. The Alexander Technique aids clients in cultivating a heightened awareness of their physical being and thought patterns, fostering a deliberate response to stimuli.

Participants engage in the Alexander Technique multiple times over the four-day retreat, gaining insights into releasing tension held within their bodies. The core principle involves learning to pause, breathe, recalibrate thoughts, and then respond. Gary emphasizes the significance of taking time to work with the myofascial of the body. Through this practice, participants develop an understanding of how to interact with the myofascial tissue, enabling a release of tension and facilitating the free flow of the divine current of the universe.

The work performed by Gary & Rob offers individuals the tools to navigate their physical and mental states, providing a pathway to open up new possibilities. The transformative impact of the Alexandar Technique is evident in the participants' journey toward self-awareness and letting go of limiting patterns.

The Journeymen Collective has developed a distinctive and purpose-driven approach to preparing individuals for shamanic ceremonies and guiding them through the integration process afterwards. Tailored for executives, entrepreneurs, and professionals, their purpose-driven journeys align with the guidance received to work with individuals influencing humanity's trajectory.
This purpose-driven journey unfolds in three phases: preparation, an intensive retreat, and integration.

The collective provides comprehensive support, offering context for potential experiences, guiding participants through the inner metaphysical planes during ceremonies, and facilitating a nuanced integration process. The intensive retreat, described as the "four seasons of Journeys," accommodates a limited number of one to four individuals, ensuring a highly personalized and attentive experience.
The intensive phase spans four full days, from morning till almost midnight, creating an immersive and transformative environment. With eyes closed for extended periods during ceremonies, participants are guided through various scenes within their psychedelic shamanic journey. The collective uniquely recalls past journeys, allowing them to assist individuals in moments of potential alignment shifts, fostering a deeper connection to the experiences.

The focus extends beyond the journey itself to the crucial integration phase. It emphasizes the importance of synthesizing, learning, understanding, and implementing insights gained during the ceremonies into daily life. Participants are encouraged to take new actions or cease activities that no longer serve them. This applied integration becomes a lifelong commitment, with individuals honouring the sacred ceremony's teachings throughout their journey of personal growth.

The choice of the name 'The Journeymen Collective' was a result of a thoughtful process during a walk in the forest. As Gary and Rob were contemplating the name of their company, the idea of guiding people on a journey with a medicine man surfaced. Recognizing that they are men, they decided to name themselves the 'Journeyman'. This name not only reflects their role as guides on a journey but also emphasizes the collective aspect of their work. The term 'Collective' signifies their mission to gather a community of individuals, fostering growth and emphasizing the concept of raising a soul community. The name 'The Journeymen Collective' encapsulates their commitment to working with everyone and uniting people under a common purpose of spiritual and personal development.

Rob and Gary advocate for the transformative power of psilocybin, specifically in the form of magic mushrooms, to facilitate a profound clearing of old energy. Their belief is grounded in the idea that mushrooms, through their mycelial networks, function as agents of decomposition and energy distribution, akin to a cleansing force in the natural environment. The

Journeymen Collective sees the use of magic mushrooms as a modern-day initiation, a reverential and sacred ceremony that has been somewhat lost in contemporary culture.

The intentional utilization of mushrooms during shamanic journeys is perceived as a unique opportunity for individuals to embark on a seven-hour journey of silence and stillness guided by Rob and Gary. This dedicated time allows participants to confront and clear karmic ties from past lives, gaining a heightened understanding of their life's purpose. The team often works with individuals already on a path of personal and spiritual development, seeking to amplify their journey by clearing unconscious habits and shadows that may be hindering progress.

The process aims to purify the individual's connection within themselves, leading to a profound recognition of universal truths such as interconnectedness and oneness. Participants are empowered to consciously engage with their minds, hearts, and gut brains, using this trifecta to process old energy and create anew. The Journeymen Collective approaches the use of magic mushrooms with deep respect, integrity, and a strong sense of intention and purpose, emphasizing the potential for a single ceremony to bring about transformative change in individuals' lives.
The Journeymen Collective shares a remarkable success story of a physician who underwent a transformative journey with them. This individual had been practising traditional Western medicine but harboured a deep desire to pursue a different path. Hindered by past trauma from his teenage years, the

physician found it challenging to step into his true purpose. Through the guidance of the Journeymen Collective, he confronted and released this lingering trauma, ultimately freeing himself to pursue his long-suppressed aspirations.

The impact was profound. The physician made significant life changes, leaving his hometown and medical career to acquire a home that now functions as a retreat centre in a completely different part of the world. Immersed in hands-on healing work, he became a respected figure in his new community, embodying the conscious impact he had always envisioned. Furthermore, he received validation from Western medicine, recognizing his unique gift and the potential to contribute to the well-being of others.

This success story is emblematic of a common trend among The Journeymen Collective's clients. As they undergo transformative journeys, individuals often experience a shift towards calmness, stillness, peace, contentment, and increased joy. They become more present, conscious of their thoughts, and adept at interpreting the signs and clues presented by the universe. The overarching theme is a profound internal transformation that enables clients to lead more fulfilling and purposeful lives.

Rob lives through his mantra for life: Reconnect to Your Soul's Remembering.

Gary lives through his mantra for life: JUST BE.

We leave you here to get inspired by this profound odyssey of self-awareness embodied by Rob and Gary and embark on our transformative journeys.
Before you close the pages of this book, brace yourselves for the rapid-fire round ahead, where insights, reflections, and the essence of their remarkable experiences await.

If you could have one gigantic billboard anywhere with anything on it, what would it say?
Rob: It would be, remember who you've come here to be.

Gary: it's on my running be.

What's one thing you are really bad at that you wish you were better at?
Rob: I think I have a lot of ideas, and I can get distracted by them. And so I'm still learning how to harness all of those horses from all the different dimensions, where there's a lot of information coming in. So that would be one thing I am really bad at.
Gary: I'm good at everything. I would love to always enhance my cooking skills because I love cooking. I've cooked all my life. So it's like, every time I'm learning something new about food and, yeah, I think that's ever-growing, ever-evolving.

So I'm not bad. I just want to get better and better and better.

Can you describe yourself in just one word?
Rob: Monadic
Gary: Steadfast.

What's your favourite thing about living in the current times, the 21st century?

Rob: My favourite thing is having people come into our centre, and I'm going to get emotional having people come into our centre and see the massive shift that takes place just in those four short days from the time that they walk into the time that they leave, and the massive level of transformation that they have. Embodied and they have access to that potent power within themselves, that they may not have had experienced before. You can see the shift on all levels. So, for me, that is my favourite thing when we have what we call our graduation dinner and just sit there and the dust has sort of settled or it's settling in and yeah, I'm just usually in awe of the level of transformation that has been embodied.

Gary: Yeah, I'd have to say the same thing. It's like, even if they haven't been on a journey with us and we meet people and they are in our presence, I mean, we're amazed at the transformation that occurs just being with us. It's not coming from ego, it's just like we're just being us and us being us, is authentic. And, that authenticity seems to let the people that we're with open up and share and learn more about themselves. Even unknowingly, they're being transformed because we get calls the next day and say, the dinner was great, but this is what happened after I left your home. And we're amazed. Those stories are just as amazing as the ones that our clients that come and experience a journey.

If you could have any superpower, what would it be and why?
Rob: Teleportation.
Gary: Well, the first game invisibility Invisible, I think that occurs sometimes.

What would be the first thing that you would do after going Invisible?
Gary: Exploration of the world is like a fly on the wall. I wonder what it would be like to be here when this conversation is happening, being in those parts of the world to see other interactions, but not be in the present, but be there. Just an observer. It's not being a spy, it's just learning from observing.

What is one electronic gadget or a fantasy gadget that you would like to see or invent yourself? Well, maybe you both have to invent.
Rob: Teleportation is like travelling to other places within the cosmos. I would also love a gadget or an electronic device that could capture the entire vision of what's transpiring inside the mind of another as they're going through a journey. So what they're seeing in the journey, I would love to be able to capture that because everybody asks us.
Gary: I think we had that ability millions of years ago, but we forgot how to tap into it. That is innate within us, where you just have to get out of the way to make it happen. a gadget.

What's your gut feeling? Is there a possibility that kind of device is going to come?
Gary: Well, if we can think of it, it probably is already being invented somewhere in the world. Somebody's

trying to create it or it's been created and it's not ready to be shared with the world.

One advice you have for our readers?
Incorporate the practice of stopping, breathing, and connecting with your heart. The guiding principle is to think with the heart and love with the mind, encapsulating the essence of a holistic and balanced approach to personal growth. The conversation is regarded as a blessing, a profound and fortunate opportunity for insightful exploration.

Question to Self:
How can you incorporate the sense of inner peace, clarity and purpose in your life?

Tune into Rob & Gary's Episode here:

8

Chitra Singh: Guiding Success, Driving Growth

Crave the path to sales excellence by nurturing Success and accelerating growth through strategic guidance and skill development

Inspired living and inspired selling can transform your life. And Chitra Singh is a living example of this. We came to know about Chitra from a dearest friend, Kavitha Garla. But after approaching Chitra and knowing her story, our exact impression of her was - a true beacon of inspiration and motivation. So this isn't just another story of a sales representative but of a woman in sales who redefined the norms of this male-dominated profile while carving a path of success for herself. Chitra is a living tale that forever changed the lives of those who crossed her path.

Chitra began her career as a medical representative for Johnson and Johnson, braving the busy streets of Mumbai day in and day out. If you have ever worked as a sales representative or know someone who did, you would know well that it isn't an easy job. You face rejection every day and yet wake up the next day to try with a better plan and different approach. Chitra did the same! Despite facing rejection and overcoming countless obstacles, remained steadfast in her determination to make a difference. It was during these challenging moments that she discovered the strength of resilience and unwavering commitment. These invaluable lessons would become the bedrock of her remarkable journey.

But this job was not it for her! Driven by an insatiable thirst for personal growth, Chitra decided to pursue an MBA at Narsee Monji, Mumbai University. This pivotal decision marked a turning point in her life, propelling her into the realm of banking sales. Guided by her passion and driven by her purpose, Chitra embarked on a journey that would span nearly three decades.

But before she celebrated her half a lifetime being in this, the ride to reach here wasn't easy by any means. In fact, it was quite a bumpy ride! The one that involves breaking stereotypes, making amends in personal and professional life, and whatnot!

The world of sales was heavily dominated by men, leaving little room for women to thrive. Undeterred by the gender imbalance, Chitra resolved to shatter the glass ceiling and pave the way for aspiring women. She became a trailblazer, leading by example and proving that success knows no gender boundaries.

Chitra's experience in sales and determination led her to establish **Saleswomentoring**, a thriving community dedicated to empowering women in sales. Through this initiative, she aimed to create a safe space for women to embrace their potential, sell with confidence, and lead with conviction. Serving as a guiding voice, Chitra provided mentorship and support to countless individuals seeking to unlock their greatness.

The journey of Saleswomentoring was not without its challenges though. Chitra had to summon the courage to step out of her comfort zone and embrace the unknown. With each obstacle she encountered, she grew stronger and wiser, discovering the transformative power of resilience, adaptability, and the ability to embrace change.
Chitra's wisdom was not limited to sales. She emphasized the importance of providing value and truly understanding the needs of customers.She understood that building strong relationships and providing exceptional experiences were crucial elements in the

world of sales. She reminded others that sales were not just transactions but opportunities to build lasting relationships and make a positive impact on the world. With her guidance, salespeople learned to listen intently, empathise deeply, and align their products or services with the genuine needs and desires of their customers.

Good salespeople, she believed, were problem solvers rather than mere product pushers.

Chitra believed in going the extra mile to ensure her clients felt valued and appreciated. She knew that entertaining clients went beyond just wining and dining; it involved creating memorable moments that would forge lasting connections. With her expertise, she shared valuable insights on how salespeople could entertain their clients effectively and differently.

First and foremost, she emphasized the significance of understanding the unique preferences and interests of each client. She encouraged salespeople to take the time to research and gather information about their client's hobbies, passions, and preferred activities. Armed with this knowledge, they could tailor their entertainment efforts to create personalized experiences.

Another key aspect that Chitra highlighted was the value of authenticity. She believed that salespeople should strive to be genuine and transparent in their interactions with clients. Rather than resorting to superficial tactics or using entertainment solely as a means to close a deal, she encouraged salespeople to focus on building trust and fostering long-term relationships. Authenticity, she believed, was the foundation of successful client entertainment.

Furthermore, Chitra stressed the significance of focusing on the journey rather than fixating solely on the destination. She encouraged breaking down goals into manageable steps and celebrating each small victory along the way. True fulfilment, she believed, lay in the pursuit of goals, not just their attainment.

Saleswomentoring stood as a testament to Chitra's unwavering commitment to empowering women in sales. Her vision extended beyond her own success, aiming to empower one million women to step into their power, unlock their potential, and create extraordinary careers. Through her inspiring journey, she instilled in others the belief that anything was possible with passion, resilience, and unwavering determination.

Chitra Singh's story served as a constant reminder that life was an ever-unfolding adventure. Within each of us lay the ability to inspire and motivate others, to transcend our circumstances, and create a lasting impact. Her voice would guide those embarking on their remarkable journey of inspired living and inspired selling. Chitra urged them to embrace their power, ignite their passion, and shape their lives and the lives of those around them.

And as you immerse yourself in Chitra's journey, we eagerly wait to share the rapid-fire round we had with her.

What is your favourite failure?
When I arrived 5 minutes late at my first job as a
Medical representative with Johnson & Johnson for a
chemist call my boss was already waiting there! He told
me a salesperson is like an actor, irrespective of the
circumstances or impediments, the salesperson has to
show up & deliver his/her lines. *We are not here to
make excuses, we are here to make a difference*.

**What are the hardships you went through while
going through your life/career journey?**
I wouldn't say they were hardships. I worked till the last
day during pregnancy in a Sales job and went back to
work when the baby was 3 months old in a new role as
a Branch Manager. The challenges were many with a
small baby at home but well, those were worth it.

What is your planned vs actual career path?
I planned to be CEO of a bank but ended up founding
my community for women to succeed at Sales -
SalesWomentoring.

What is the turning point in your life?
When I left my corporate job after nearly 3 decades in
Banking, I realised I wanted to multiply & amplify my
impact by encouraging women to be confident
negotiators and combat the traditional biases which
dominate the world women live & work in. So I founded
a community for women to encourage them to be
confident Sellers.

Who influenced you the most & how?
My Father always encouraged me to speak my mind &
fight for what I believed in. Fight for equality & a fair
world for women.

**What is that one incident that transformed your
life?**
When my mother passed away I realised that no
amount of money can bring back a human life. Hence
decided to focus on creating impact & transforming
lives rather than making more & more money.

**What is one thing you would do differently in the
past?**
No regrets.

**What is your Vision/Goal/ in life and what are you
trying to achieve?**
My purpose is to provide an ecosystem to enable 1
million women to sell with confidence through my
community **SalesWomentoring** - India's only
community Inspiring women to succeed at Selling.

**What is the craziest/naughtiest thing you have done
in childhood?**
Caught stray dogs & bathed them to clean them up
...almost drowned them.

**What is one hidden/unknown/least known fact
about you?**
I am a singer & poet.

What's your favourite fantasy gadget that you want for yourself/want to invent?
Time machine.

If you are not at work, what do you like doing?
Exercising & singing.

How do you keep yourself up-to-date? Please share links or references to websites/blogs/books etc.
Simon Sinek's books, and Shari Levitin's videos on LinkedIn.

What is one piece of advice you want to give to the youngsters in the field?
Be curious, be confident, be coachable, have clarity about your goals & be committed to investing time /effort in achieving your goals (5 C's).

What are your thoughts about The Guiding Voice platform?
Brilliant platform to coach students, entrepreneurs & IT professionals. Practical & simple tips on life & work and of course amazing guests.

One Quote or Anecdote that you strongly believe in?
The bridge between who you are and who you can be is - Confidence ~Chitra Singh.

> **Question to Self:**
> How am I approaching competition and collaboration in my profession? Does it contribute to a broader shift in attitudes and opportunities for individuals in the field?

Tune into Chitra's Episode here:

9

E Prabhakar Reddy: A Fearless Educationist Nurturing Creativity, Resilience, and Empathy

A journey ignited on September 5th and fuelled by the principles of education, dedication, and the indomitable human spirit.

In the embrace of time, where the echoes of wisdom and experience resonate, there are individuals who traverse landscapes of dedication and vision, weaving tales that touch lives in profound ways. This book - ***The Guiding Voice Inspiring Lives Volume 2*** - is all about them. Their stories, like constellations in the night sky, illuminate paths for those who follow.

September 5th, a date hallowed in the realm of education, stands as a symbol of such narratives—a date that educators worldwide hold close to their hearts. Something happened on this very day, in the year 2003. Naveen's professional odyssey commenced- parallel to India's celebration of Teachers' Day. It was the inception of a journey entwined with the principles imprinted by a remarkable teacher. As he reflects upon his School Principal and English faculty, while writing this, the image of Mr. Prabhakar Reddy emerges from the tapestry of his memories- a figure whose life's chronicle transcends the confines of time. Mr. Prabhakar Reddy's story is an embodiment of inspiration, resilience, and the transformational power of education.

Mr. Prabhakar Reddy, a revered educationist in Telangana, India, possesses over four decades of experience in running educational institutions. He exemplifies the true essence of a teacher, having guided thousands of students towards successful careers, entrepreneurial ventures, and leadership roles around the world. But before we talk of his achievements, we want you to know him better.

Born into a humble agrarian household, Mr. Reddy imbibed the virtues of integrity and diligence from his father, a man resolute in his principles. Despite the challenges they encountered, his father emphasized the value of labour and the pursuit of excellence. These rudimentary lessons later underpin the fabric of Mr. Reddy's expedition.

Mr Reddy's journey to discipline and punctuality began at a Government school as National Cadet Corps during his college year. It is not an overstatement to say that these years set his trajectory toward success. The NCC experience taught him the art of unwavering perseverance, completing tasks with dedication, and embracing the essence of professionalism. Supported by the same environment at home, Mr. Reddy just moved up and beyond from here.

Having been blessed with mentors serving as role models for him, he made a decision in the career he desired and proposed to pursue a career in teaching. His mentors, paragons of inspiration, kindled his ambition to embrace pedagogy—an ardour that remains undiminished.

When Mr. Reddy transitioned to the city to start his journey as an educationist, the urban landscape revealed to him the chasm between government and private institutions. At this stage, he just recalled the profound impact his teachers had on his life and decided to transform the lives of young individuals in the same way. Inspired by Sri Aurobindo Ghosh's[2]

---

[2] *https://en.wikipedia.org/wiki/Sri_Aurobindo

ideals, he erected the edifice of Sri Aurobindo High School, an embodiment of Aurobindo's educational vision.

Thus began the journey of Sri Aurobindo High School, at Jangaon, a small rural town at that time with humble origins. This was fuelled by the support of remarkable individuals and parents who recognized the school's commitment to delivering quality education. Through their labour and fidelity, the institution attained eminence, emblematic of its principles, ethics, and scholarly prowess. These beginnings are just Mr Reddy's steadfast resolve to ensure an equitable education for every class of society.

But his journey to this establishment was not a straight road. It was a bumpy ride full of external elements aiming to undermine his endeavours. He was disseminated with false allegations to sully his reputation. Yet, his resolve remained undeterred, like a sentinel guarding his vision, committed to the advancement of his wards.

The culmination of Mr Reddy's educational pursuits materialized when his disciple, Deepa Yerravelli, earned 7th rank in the entire state in 1997. This milestone not only swelled the institution's pride but bolstered the conviction that relentless labour, coupled with inspired instruction, could uncover the latent potential in every student.

As of today, Sri Aurobindo High School is known for creating a trail of distinction. A 100% graduation rate became its hallmark, a conveyor belt of accomplished graduates.

Mr Reddy's unswerving dedication to perpetual refinement and his ability to ignite teachers and scholars alike steered the trajectory of this achievement.

Amid the shifting sands of education, Mr. Reddy vouches for adaptability. He perceives a teacher's role as an anchor in a student's life that extends beyond education. With the student already being loaded with knowledge resources, a teacher's role is critical in nurturing critical analysis, problem-solving, and a lifelong ardour for learning. With mentors' guidance, scholars can reach their highest potential.

The bedrock of a child's education and overall development is, Mr. Reddy affirms, the parents. He urges parents to be actively involved in their child's learning journey, fostering a strong bond and providing support. By understanding each child's unique potential, parents can become torchbearers, explore diverse career paths and help them make informed decisions for their future.

In a world where herd mentality and social conformity prevail, Mr. Reddy encourages parents to embrace individuality and nurture their children's dreams. He advises against imposing societal expectations and instead encourages parents to listen, guide, and empower their children to become compassionate, creative, and resilient individuals.

It is probably the joint effort of educationists like Mr. Reddy that physical punishments in school are a thing of the past. The education landscape has evolved to provide student counselling and focus on behavioural correction. We don't deny this either! The emphasis on discipline through affirmative reinforcement and right mentorship goes a long way.

While this is a tale of an educator whose influence extends beyond the classroom, transcending generations and boundaries, we continue to navigate through the chapters of his life. And witnessed not only the transformation of a community but the metamorphosis of an individual—a journey ignited on September 5th and fueled by the principles of education, dedication, and the indomitable human spirit.

And now here is us exploring the fun side of this educationist and learning from his life anecdotes.

What is your favourite failure?
I aimed to become a pilot and failed. This made me run educational institutions that shaped 1000s of students who are now very well settled in successful positions across the globe.

Any hardships you went through in your life/career journey?
Almost every ascent I stalked.

What is the major turning point of your life?
It was a friend's suggestion- to establish a school.

One person that influenced you the most & how?
My father, by his determined decisions.

One incident that transformed your life?
Joining Sri Aurobindo organization.

One thing you would have done differently in the past.
I have been passionate about farming and wanted to do something in it.

If you are not at work, what do you like doing?
I love getting involved in agriculture.

What is one piece of advice you want to give to the youngsters in the field?
Truthful life is the hardest, but you reap delicious fruits.

What are your thoughts about The Guiding Voice platform?
It is an excellent platform to guide individuals.

One quote or Anecdote that you strongly believe in? (It may be your own quote or something that resonated with you)
Don't be self-centred. Be selfless as much as possible.

> **Question to Self:**
> How does this story challenge my perspectives on
> education, privilege, and social responsibility?

Tune into Mr. Prabhakar Reddy's English Episode here:

10

Alex Bennett: Discovering His Passion & Breaking Norms

What if there's more to life than simply going through the motions?

Have you ever caught yourself in a whirlwind of routines and responsibilities? Following the well-trodden path that society expects of us. For some of us, it is the force of situations and for others, the conscious choice we make every day. Maybe because of the predictability and security it provides us?

But we at TGV often wonder if the key to true fulfilment lies in our ability to recognize our passions and take bold steps to pursue them. And each guest, whoever was a part, believed in themselves to create a dent by just listening to their heart.

Our recent guest on the TGV podcast was Alex Bennett. From a secured, well-paying job, he decided to risk it all and followed his passion for opening up a Restaurant and bar. For him this was challenging the status quo, unleashing his inner aspirations, and embarking on a journey toward a life filled with purpose and passion.

Alex Bennett's journey through life has been shaped by his experiences as a bartender and restaurateur, where he's honed invaluable life skills that extend far beyond the confines of his profession. In the journey, he explored three core lessons that have guided Alex's life and continued to drive his pursuit of passion: ***patience, active listening, and unwavering focus.*** These lessons, he believes, are not only applicable to the service industry but also to anyone seeking fulfilment and success in their unique way.

As we had a conversation with Alex on his life philosophies and to understand the deeper meaning behind it, he walked us through what it meant for him to pursue the above three in his life's journey:

Patience: Letting Life Unfold

At the heart of Alex's life philosophy is patience. His years working in the hustle and bustle of the restaurant industry have taught him that in both the micro-moments and larger life decisions, patience is key. It's about stepping back, taking a breath, and allowing life to work itself out. Alex urges us not to become slaves to our emotions, emphasizing that a calm and patient approach often yields the most favourable outcomes.

Listening: The Art of Connection

One of the most crucial skills developed over the years is being a good listener. Being a person behind the tables he realised that it is not just about taking orders in a restaurant but also about connecting with people. You want to get to know people, you want to be a conversationalist. As the Greek philosopher's saying goes, ***"Man has two ears but one tongue so that he can listen twice as much as he speaks."*** Alex's approach with each customer who shows up at his restaurant is to build meaningful relationships by truly engaging in conversations and showing a genuine interest in their stories.

Focus: Staying on Course

Amid the restaurant industry's chaos, Alex stresses the need for focus. He gives a restaurant analogy that if eight tables are going at one time and you got one bad table it could throw you off and you lose focus. Leading to ruining the experience for seven other tables. But if you maintain your focus, then it won't affect you and you will still try to give the best experience to the other tables. Alex's advice is clear: don't get sidetracked by the minutiae. By maintaining your focus, you can better navigate life's challenges and achieve success even in the face of adversity.

As impressed as we were with these basic yet fundamental life lessons coming from Alex, we sought his viewpoint further for anyone who is trying to make a career in the restaurant and bar industry. His first and foremost advice is - to *be a people person! **A successful restaurant runs on the idea of investing in people and getting to know people.*** A happy customer not only gives your restaurant a profit margin but also gives you a purpose to show up every day. And if you are driven by purpose, everything else falls into place.

Alex's journey in the restaurant industry reveals a crucial life lesson: success often lies in pursuing your passion rather than chasing money.

In a world where financial gain is often prioritised, he suggests that finding your purpose and investing in people can lead to a more fulfilling life. His experience demonstrates that celebrating with friends and connecting with customers can bring joy even in the face of challenges.

Alex's transition from bartending to writing offers additional insights. The three valuable lessons he shared also highlight his writing process. He stresses that writing is a gradual process, where the first draft is bound to be imperfect. So, the key is to get your thoughts on paper first and refine them later. Drawing stories from personal experiences makes storytelling more relatable and allows for authenticity in your work.

In the fabric of life's teachings, one particular thread stands out as an enduring piece of wisdom from this sage bartender, Alex Bennett. His profound advice is to keep an open mind.

Alex's words remind us that our own biases, prejudices, and preconceived notions can often obscure our path to growth and understanding. The beauty lies in those unexpected conversations with patrons from all walks of life, offering fresh outlooks on the world. Through this lens of an open mind, one can uncover new layers of insight, and personal growth takes root. Life, as Alex puts it, has a way of surprising us when we pause to listen, truly listen, to the stories that unfold in front of us.

As Alex relates these lessons from his life in every aspect of what he does, we begin to see the broader applications of these principles too. Patience, active listening, and unwavering focus are virtues that can be harnessed by anyone seeking purpose and success. Whether you are in the service industry, pursuing an artistic endeavour, or navigating the corporate world, these lessons are universal, helping you find your path and reach your full potential.

Before you dive into the thoughts, let's take a moment to explore Alex's life from a different perspective. We're about to enter the "Rapid Fire Round," a quick series of questions designed to provide a glimpse into the man behind the bar.

If you could have any gigantic billboard anywhere and with anything on it, what would it say?
Probably, buy my book! I say I'm a living billboard in that respect, and I am going to be selling my book for the rest of my life.

What's one thing you are bad at, that you wish you were better or good at?
I wish I could learn another language. I've tried. And I work in restaurants, I work in kitchens. I work with a lot of native Spanish speakers, and I picked up a little bit here and there. But you have to think in the language, and I just can't do it.

Describe yourself in just one word?
Authentic: What you see is what you get.

What is your favourite failure?
When I have someone come into my bar who has just gone through a break-up, I often advise them to try something their former significant other would have never supported them doing. For me, it was playing the guitar and, determined to learn it, I took lessons for six months. However, after six months I realized, I was much better at listening to music than I would ever be at playing it. But that's ok—I never wonder anymore whether I would've been a rock star and I now have a healthier respect for musicians.

What is your favourite thing about living in the current times?
I would say fresh water!
I appreciate what that means for us in terms of you can go to a sink, turn on the spigot and take a Drink and it's

safe. There are a lot of places in the world where it's still not like that, and you're walking a mile every day to fill up two buckets with fresh water. We are blessed to not go out and hunt.

If you could have any superpower, what would it be and why?
I'd say, invisibility.
I'm a listener, so if I could be in a room that nobody knows I'm in that room and listen to what they're saying. And I have been in that situation a lot of times at the bar too. You often hear people talking about stuff that is interesting and they kind of open up in a way. So, I would love to be invisible and listen to those conversations.

What are the hardships you went through while going through your life/career journey?
I got divorced in my early thirties and I will say that was one of the toughest phases of my life. When I got married, I had a certain perception of what my future would hold. Then, suddenly, I found myself having to change everything I thought was going to happen and start over. In the end, though, I'm glad it worked out the way it did because I grew as a person and met people who I would've never met, and they became my best friends. It later inspired me to write the book.

Another hardship happened in my early forties when my health took a turn for the worst. I had always suffered from mild psoriasis/eczema but suddenly my symptoms grew exponentially worse and made my life miserable. As a result, I had to completely rethink my approach to my health. Now, in my fifties, I consider that experience a good thing because I had to confront my poor lifestyle choices and I'm in better shape today because of it.

What is your planned vs actual career path?
My parents bought a restaurant when I was sixteen and I always thought I'd be a part of it. Then they sold it to my in-laws, who became my former in-laws, and it changed my life course forever. I then went back to school and earned my Masters in Education with the intention of teaching English but the collapse of the housing market in 2010 made it impossible to find a job and I settled in as a full-time bartender. Thank God it worked out the way it did. I made friends with a diverse group of people who would inspire me to grow as a person and encourage me to write. Now, as I enter a new chapter in my life, I feel I'm well prepared for the journey and I'm looking forward to seeing where it takes me.

Who is one person that influenced you the most & how?
Being a bartender, I've been blessed to get exposed to a diverse amount of people who all contributed to my success in some way. Therefore, I can't pick any one person. I'd have to say, beyond my close friends and family, my regulars and my coworkers inspire me every day.

What is one incident that transformed your life?
Experiencing health issues taught me to appreciate the little things in life and to stay in the moment as much as possible.

What is the one thing you would do differently in the past?
I would've been more in the moment with my boys when they were younger and enjoyed their childhood.

What is your Vision/Goal/ in life?
As much as I enjoy bartending and growing up being a bartender, I would love to have my book take me around the world. I want to see the world and learn from different people and cultures.

What is one hidden/unknown/least known fact about you?
I love flower gardening and wish to spend more time doing it.

What is one favourite fantasy gadget that you want for yourself/want to invent?
A way to immediately analyse food to know if it is safe for me to eat and won't set off a skin reaction.

If you are not at work, what do you like doing?
I'm a big fantasy baseball guy and I love listening to games on the radio when I have a pitcher on the mound. I found something about the cadence very relaxing.

One piece of advice you want to give to the youngsters in the field.
Keep an open mind. An open mind is a learning mind and once we stop learning, we start dying.

What are your thoughts about The Guiding Voice platform?
I think it's awesome! With all the negativity in the world, it can be hard to be positive, but I feel like The Guiding Voice provides a place where people inspire each other and one can gain valuable insight on ways to improve their lives and careers.

One quote or Anecdote that you strongly believe in.
"Man has two ears but one tongue and that is so he can listen to twice as much as he speaks".
~Epictetus

<table><tr><td>Question to Self:
How can I infuse more passion and connection into my pursuits?</td></tr></table>

Tune into Alex's Episode here:

11

Ramesh Manickavel: A resilient leader, artist, and mentor

Extraordinary journey of a visionary leader and trailblazer who has inspiring achievements, unwavering determination, and transformative impact, as he defies odds and paves the way for innovation and success".

Despite facing challenges in his personal life, he has dedicated himself to nurturing young talent and empowering them to reach their full potential. Ramesh Manickavel's journey is about his unwavering commitment and belief in the transformative power of mentorship.

A few years ago Ramesh's life took an unexpected turn. It was a battle that tested his strength, both physically and emotionally. But Ramesh refused to let the thing define him. With unwavering determination, he faced the challenges head-on and triumphed over adversity. His experience shaped his perspective on life, teaching him the value of every moment and the importance of pursuing his dreams - and art was his calling!

As Ramesh embarked on his artistic journey, it became his solace and a medium through which he could express his emotions and experiences. With every stroke of the paintbrush and pencil, he breathed life into his thoughts, creating breathtaking artwork. There was no limit to Ramesh's artistic exploration. His sketches and paintings ranged from a child deep in thought, reflecting the innocence of youth, to the serene face of Lord Buddha, capturing the essence of enlightenment. He also drew inspiration from various prominent Indian temples, capturing their intricate architecture and spiritual significance. Ramesh's creativity knew no boundaries, and he even found beauty in the simplest things, like a half-peeled orange or his favourite spot at work.

But Ramesh's journey was not only about his personal artistic growth. He became a mentor to young talents, eager to pass on his knowledge and inspire others to pursue their creative passions. His infectious passion and belief in the power of art motivated and uplifted those around him. Through his mentorship, Ramesh nurtured the next generation of creative minds, instilling in them the same values of perseverance and the pursuit of dreams that guided him throughout his journey.

As Ramesh Manickavel's extraordinary journey continued, he became a beacon of hope and inspiration for all those who crossed his path. His story served as a reminder that no matter the challenges one faces, with determination, creativity, and mentorship, one can overcome any obstacle and leave a transformative impact on the world.

"We are what we think. All that we are arises from our thoughts. With our thoughts, we make the world." ~Buddha

"What do you want to be when you grow up?"

"Kind", said the boy.

Charlie Mackesy, from the book "**The Boy, the Mole, the Fox and the Horse**"

And solitude is not isolation. I can't believe how one of my favourite sketches matched with one of my all-time favourite background scores by Ilayaraja[3] sir.

I live in that solitude which is painful in youth, but delicious in the years of maturity. ~Albert Einstein

Baidyanath, Jharkhand

---

[3] https://en.wikipedia.org/wiki/Ilaiyaraaja

Poetry of brush meets the poetry of architecture. Charminar in Sumi-e style.

Art has the transformative power of healing, self-expression, and connecting with others.

Behind every mask, there is a face, and behind that a story.

His passion for spiderman was so high that he didn't realise he had flu when he drew this. Though he was extremely tired and couldn't even get up from bed. But sketched the three Spider-Man coming together. This sketch is a perfect example of how passion can soothe you, comfort you and eventually heal you.

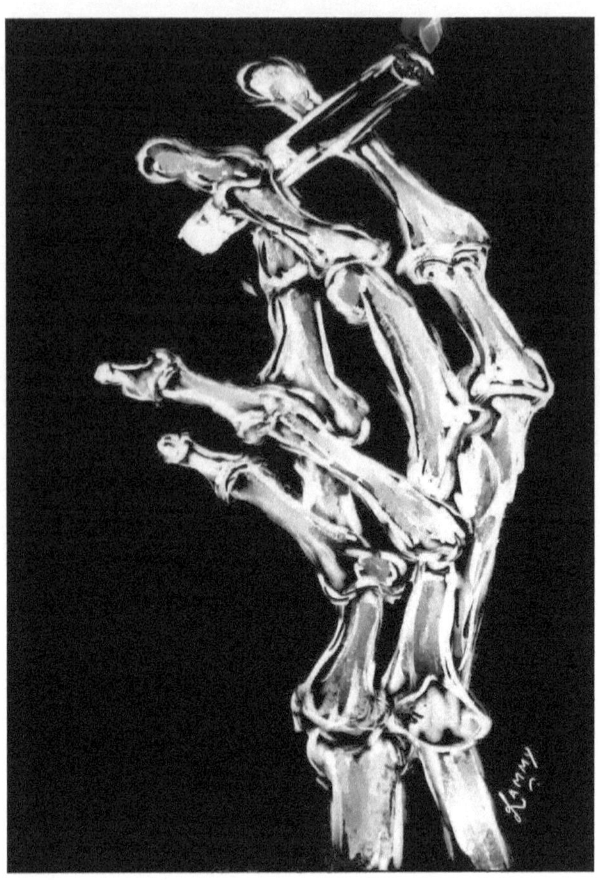

Before smoking, think about your loved ones.
Before smoking, think about yourself.
YOU are precious!

"You're a precious hidden diamond, sunken in mud" ~Rumi

Stepping onto the campus of Madurai American College was a dream come true for Ramesh Manickavel, albeit in a different capacity than he had originally envisioned. Years ago, financial constraints prevented him from attending the college, but he would often pause and admire the beautiful campus and aspiring students whenever he passed by. Ramesh's father, thrilled when he finally gained admission, would proudly drop him off on his bicycle each day, his words filled with paternal pride.

Emotions overwhelmed Ramesh as he recently found himself back on the same campus, not as a student, but as a speaker at the International Conference on Data Transformation. He was certain his father was watching over him with immense pride. During his session, Ramesh covered a range of key topics, from innovation in AI and threats to cyber security to job opportunities, global recession, automation, and the profound influence of ChatGPT in various fields. While he delved into the technical aspects that students should learn and master, he emphasized the importance of preserving individualism while pursuing their dreams.

Ramesh had always harboured a desire to co-author an article with a student, and his wish came true when he collaborated with Celina Daisy J., a final-year MCA student at American College. Little did Ramesh know the remarkable journey that lay ahead when Celina chose spam classification as her final year project. Together, they explored various learning algorithms, extending beyond the confines of supervised learning, the conventional approach to spam classification.

This experience exemplified one of the countless instances where Ramesh had transformed the lives of students hailing from tier 2 towns and underprivileged backgrounds. His dedication to nurturing young talent knew no bounds.

While Ramesh preferred not to publicize his non-profit organization, Anand Memorial Trust, on social platforms, he openly shared his recent visit to the Sphoorti Akshara Yagnam Study centres. During his visit, he witnessed the power of teamwork, exceptional coordination, and inspirational leadership. These study centres, located in impoverished neighbourhoods, were established to provide after-school services to children. Anand Memorial Trust, through its educational and financial assistance programs, aimed to empower the excellence of youth.

Their primary motto, "***Be a reason for someone's smile***," drove their commitment to supporting educational and cultural development, providing relief to the underprivileged, and promoting social welfare. The collaboration with Sphoorti Akshara Yagnam study centres had been ongoing for several months, with virtual interactions and brainstorming sessions to explore various means of support. However, this visit marked Ramesh's first opportunity to witness the impact firsthand.

The purpose of Ramesh's trip was to meet the children in person, to understand how the study centres were helping them, and how he could further support their endeavours. The study centres not only aimed to create an environment conducive to learning for underprivileged children but also meticulously analysed the entire ecosystem to provide a better overall experience. One notable focus area involved training the parents in vocational programs, ultimately enhancing their financial stability. Ramesh was moved by the stories and witnessed the newfound confidence in women who had undergone the tailoring courses organized by the organization.

Witnessing college students step forward to teach and support the children truly exemplified the concept of paying it forward. Their level of maturity and willingness to contribute to society mirrored the support they had received in their own lives. During the certificate distribution ceremony for the tailoring program, the children praised their teacher, Aruna. In response, Aruna humbly shared that someone had trusted and helped her in the past, and she was simply perpetuating that kindness to the best of her ability.

As the number of children joining the centres increased, a shortage of bags and snacks became evident. Despite the best planning efforts, there simply weren't enough resources to go around. However, what unfolded next showcased the true spirit of compassion and generosity. The existing children, who had already received their bags, willingly and selflessly offered them to those who hadn't yet gotten theirs. It was a heartwarming sight to behold, witnessing these young souls giving the only things they had to bring smiles to their new friends' faces. In that simple act of sharing care, they exemplified the true meaning of empathy and the power of unity.

Meanwhile, behind the scenes, a remarkable coordination effort was underway to ensure the smooth functioning of the 52 centres and the well-being of the

1,250 children they served. This endeavour was known as the "Scrum of Scrum", an aptly named approach that employed modern technologies like WhatsApp to facilitate seamless communication and collaboration. Hemasekhar Marupuri, the Secretary of the Social Integrated Rural Development Society and Director of Sphoorti Foundation, together with the unwavering support of Srivyal Vuyyuri, the Founder of Sphoorti, and Tejaswini Vavilala, the Program Director of Sphoorti, had built an incredible coordination and feedback system. Through this system, the daily status of attendance, activities, and challenges were shared, enabling the coordinators from each cluster to highlight the obstacles they faced. This remarkable display of teamwork and coordination ensured that the centres continued to thrive and make a lasting impact on the lives of the children.

Amid this network of care and support, Ramesh Manickavel, a driving force behind the Anand Memorial Trust, realized that the organization received more than it gave. The trust had been providing support in every possible way, but the impact it had on Ramesh's own heart surpassed anything they could have imagined. His recent visit to the study centres filled his being with an overwhelming sense of gratitude and love. As he returned from the centres, he carried with him the words of his favourite poet, Rumi, who said,
"You are not a drop in the ocean; you are the entire ocean in a drop."

Ramesh recognized that each one of us possesses the power to create a significant impact, no matter the size of our contribution. Whether it was supporting a centre, sponsoring a child's education, or providing study materials, he knew that every act of kindness and support would help turn the children's dreams into reality.

Ramesh has proved that to create a difference, you do not need a lot of monetary investment. But willpower and optimal use of your skills is the key to success here.

And while we leave you to process and take some inspiration from Ramesh, here is the fun-filled rapid-fire round to make you meet the other side of Ramesh Manickavel

What is your favourite failure?
In my opinion, there is no such thing as failure. At times despite our best efforts, we may not get the desired results. I was preparing hard to join my favourite Engineering College. However, I couldn't write the entrance exam for which I had put in all my efforts for two years. I was feeling low for a long time. But looking back, this is one of my favourite lessons. No matter our effort and dedication, there are few things beyond our control. Instead of beating ourselves for things that we couldn't achieve, I learned to pat on my back because I had given my best and that's all that matters.

What are the Hardships you went through while going through your life/career journey?
For a short period during my career, I had to take care of my dad's business (which involved a lot of travel and sleepless nights) since he was bedridden. It was extremely hard for me to focus on my work and travel. I

realized my dad had been doing this for a long time and never complained or even let his family know the pain involved. This taught me a lot of life lessons, especially the gratitude for everything we receive no matter how tiny they are.

What is the major turning point in your life?
There are too many to list. However, the pattern is similar, in most of them it's about getting something very different from what I wanted. Though they were disappointing initially, when I look back on the challenges I had to steer through because of such changes, I consider them as blessings in my life. To give one major turning point, I wanted to join my dream college but it didn't happen. I accepted what came in my path. I am not sure how my life would have been if I was able to get the degree in the college I wanted to study, I feel blessed and grateful for where I am.

Who is that one person who influenced you the most & how?
Bharath Kalyanram doesn't need an introduction. I have been fortunate to start my career with him. There are so many wonderful traits about Bharath but the topmost that comes to my mind is how he treats people with utmost respect and kindness. As a leader, his mantra is to walk the talk and he leads by example.

What is that one incident that transformed your life?
A few years ago, one day rumours were spreading that could potentially create a problem for the involved people. I felt proud of not spreading it any further and advising my friends not to spread it either. After

listening to the entire incident, my mentor told me that I still was part of the problem because I didn't try to address the root cause of the issue in my capacity. I ignored the problem and was more focused on not getting associated with it without even understanding my ability to solve the issue. That incident taught me the leap of leadership, that extra step that differentiates an individual from the leader. This transformed me to be a better person by asking '***What else can I do to help?***' in everything I do.

What is the one thing you would do differently in the past?
If I get a chance to do time travel, to see whatever I did, I would do it all over again (absolutely no regrets) but I would slow down, enjoy the moment and be kind to myself.

What is your Vision/Goal/ in life and what are you trying to achieve?
'Education for all' – the topmost vision with which we started our 'Anand Memorial Trust'. I have two related goals with this: One is to be able to support education for underprivileged kids and to be able to provide education that teaches life skills.

What is the craziest/naughtiest thing you have done in childhood?
I frequently ran away from home to escape from the scolding for the problems I had created. Looking back it amazes me how fearlessly I have gone to places where I had no idea at all and the confidence I had in getting back despite all the troubles I caused.

What is one hidden/unknown/least known fact about you?
I guess most of my friends now know that I can sketch. So that's not a hidden fact about me anymore. Let me share something I found about myself recently. As much as I like to interact with people, there are times I like to be on my own. I learned that there is a name to it and I am an ambivert!

Which is your favourite fantasy gadget, that you want for yourself/want to invent?
Being a hardcore fan of Spider-Man, the ability to spin a web is my all-time fantasy and who knows – anything and everything is possible.

If you are not at work, what do you like doing?
Art is therapy to me. Though ink and watercolour are my favourite mediums, I experiment with different ways of sketching and I enjoy the flow. I am quite active in the SketchADay app which is exclusively for folks who are passionate about drawing and I can't believe I have drawn 905 sketches as of today.

How do you keep yourself up-to-date? Please share links or references to websites/blogs/books etc.
1. Talking to people, especially students. I learned so much from them. I had to learn PUBG to be able to teach simulation and prescriptive analytics and believe me, it was so much fun!
2. The world of Data Science fascinates me and I feel the field is evolving every day. I am an avid follower of the sites:
https://www.analyticsvidhya.com/
https://towardsdatascience.com/

3. "***To be able to teach, one has to learn first***" is something I firmly believe. For most of the topics, I learn from W3Schools Online Web Tutorials as well as Udemy courses.

One piece of advice you want to give to the youngsters in the field.
It is okay if the things you aspire for are not working out the way you wanted them to. Please don't be hard on yourself for things that are not in your control and please be kind to whom you see in the mirror.

What are your thoughts about The Guiding Voice platform?
In one word, it's a "***blessing***". The name is so apt for the purpose – of guiding, no matter who you are and what stage of life/career/passion you are in. I am amazed at the undivided focus and attention and so glad to see where TGV has reached today and the journey ahead. Whatever topics/subjects I can think of there is a podcast already out there. I am so privileged to be part of it, even if it is the tiniest.

Quote or Anecdote that you strongly believe in?
"***What you seek is seeking you***" –law of attraction. It's okay to listen to our intuition no matter how silly it may sound, it's okay to follow our dreams and pursue our passion no matter how impossible they may seem to be because what we seek is also seeking us.

<table>
<tr><td>

Question to self:
Q. What can I contribute to creating a positive impact in society?

</td></tr>
</table>

Tune into Ramesh (Rammy)'s Episode here:

12

Suman De: A Techie's Expedition to Explore New Horizons with Research

Have you ever read a research paper that left you feeling inspired, intrigued or even a little awestruck?

Perhaps it presented a groundbreaking new theory, challenged long-held assumptions, or offered a glimpse into an exciting new field of study. Whatever the subject matter, a well-written research paper has the power to captivate readers and inspire new ideas and approaches to the challenges we face.

We recently read one, and it was from a Techie!

Whoever has interacted with the co-author of this book, Naveen Samala knows for a fact that he is a well-informed person. If not, he is inquisitive enough to learn about a subject. Here's another interesting thing about Naveen, in the era of the Digital world, he still prefers to read Newspapers!

Wondering What about it?
Well, on a random Wednesday morning when Naveen picked up the newspaper, his eye caught a young techie's blurb in it. A section where he shared about his company, SAP India- culture, work environment, research, etc. And Naveen did what he does best! Reached out to him on LinkedIn in a fraction of a second. And while he was quick with reaching out, Suman, at the other end of this connection was quick in responding, and from here started the curiosity to know Suman De and his published work.

Suman by profession is a Software Development Specialist with SAP India for the past 8+ years. A techie, like many of us! But here's the catch - Suman De is also an IEEE (Institute of Electrical and Electronics Engineers) Member with 15+ Research Papers published in his name. Including a book chapter on cyber security. All when he wasn't even planning to pursue a PhD.

We know what you are thinking!
How a techie is making a name in research while being in corporate?
As much as we understand - Tech is 'making things happen' and Papers have 'theory on how to make it happen' - so yes, they do meet at a common point! And while we talk more on the 'how it happens' part, this chapter in our book is also going to inspire you to write and become a published Research Paper author yourself. Because as Suman describes it, anyone can do it! All you need is a blend of innovative thinking and the patience to write it down.

Suman's journey and curiosity started way back when he was doing his bachelor's degree in computer applications. In the final year of project submission, his mentor suggested not to follow the obvious path of developing an application, scoring marks and leaving the college, but to come up with an idea sourced from the already existing tech. Write a research paper, get it published and then work on that idea to build the application. For most, college is just to get a degree and move forward with a high-paying package. But for Suman, it served more than that. He wrote 2 papers in his final year on encryption of cloud security which also made space in an international journal.

It was just a start for Suman! But the journey wasn't as straightforward as it may sound.

After his college, Suman got a job with SAP India - which was his dream company. His promising 8 years with the company explain well that he lived his dream. But this was not all that Suman wanted. His passion for writing (and dream of becoming a journalist since childhood!) made him go back to writing papers. And thanks to the Pandemic of 2020 he got a good amount of time on his hands to write. So, after a break of 3.5 years, Suman restarted writing Research Papers and published over 8 papers in a single year. His favourite amongst all is a paper on 'Resource Conflict Management using Graph Theory'. An algorithm that reduces the waiting time of a project by allocating the resources effectively across units. This is a great help to organizations that have a single individual involved in multiple projects. Besides the effectiveness of the solution, this topic is close to Suman's heart because of his college Professor. Graph Theory was a topic his professor researched and writing this paper was Suman's way to pay tribute to him. This made us only think of the quote, ***Things done with honesty do have an impact on society***. Research papers written by Suman made him a thought leader in the tech industry, where he continues to inspire thousands of individuals out there.

Being a techie, Suman was aware and updated about the happenings in tech. Logically, every tech out there first started on paper. An idea was there. Someone read it. Got another idea from it. And suggested it in the form of another research paper, building the base on all available facts. The closer you are to working with the customer, the more aware you are of the gap in the industry. An idea suggested by you to fill the gap can go a long way in the form of a research paper. Nevertheless, there could also be a patent on your name if you develop that solution.

As insightful as it was having this conversation with Suman, a lot of our pondering was on the thought - where do you start?
So, we reached out to our expert, and here is what he has to say-

"Read everything possible around the subject - Journals, Magazines, Books, etc. Hit the Google search for upcoming and trending tech in that field. Once you are through with where the tech stands, find the loophole. Come up with your creative solution to it and get into writing it down."

While all this might sound like a daunting task, once something holds your interest, it becomes a cakewalk. For non-techies planning to get into this - pick a field of your interest, compare what's out there and come up with what you think can be done.

One piece of advice Suman De has for all those who want to start their journey of writing a research paper is to start by reading what other researchers have written. Do a literature survey. Pick your topic of interest and read everything on it that happened in the past 3-4 years and ask 3 questions - **What, Why and How.**
What is the problem statement?
Why is it considered?
How are they solving it?

Answer these three before writing a paper. And once you are done, figure out the open problems they have left. Try solving it on your own and prove why your solution is the best.

Here we leave you inspired by the thought of having your paper published someday. And now is the time to make you meet the crazy side of this techie with a fun rapid fire.

What is your most memorable moment so far?
My most memorable moment was clearing SAP interviews 8 years ago.

What do you want to become in your next life?
Steve Jobs! For this life, I am adapting his signature Turtleneck T-shirts.

What is your favourite failure?
My favourite failure was not qualifying or getting a decent rank in any of the major Engineering Entrances. That helped me chart a different path for myself. The failure made it simpler for me to focus on what I was good at rather than following the crowd doing BTech. I knew my interest was always in solving problems (not maths ;) but through code).

As we grow, situations only get tougher, but now I prefer exploring alternate routes than simply taking what seems simpler and obvious.

Would you like to share some hardships you went through in your life/career journey?
Coming from a lower-middle-class family has its challenges, and they are not just financial. When knowledge and money are both limited, we learn how to work hard and manage finances in ways we didn't even imagine before. I had just spent 4222/- rupees in my first month in Bangalore, and this might seem unbelievable in 2015, but something I take pride in. Growing my career with SAP addressed both, and looking back at my college and working student days between 2012 - 2018, gives me a sense of satisfaction that I went through that phase and moulded my character.

What is one animal you relate with the most?
Owl, for sure! Because I love to burn the midnight oil

What is the best compliment you have ever received?
This is from my Engineering days when a college Professor used to criticise me a lot. But on the date of the project submission, he said in front of the entire class that "this person is logically better than me".

What have you dreamt of becoming in childhood?
I wanted to be a journalist.

What is one thing you want to change from your past?
I could have started playing football at 10 instead of playing it in college for a start.

What is one Hidden/unknown/least known fact about you?
I love to cook! Not many people are aware, but weekends are best spent experimenting in the kitchen.

Favourite fantasy gadget that you want for yourself/want to invent.
A Transporter (refer to Star Trek)

If you are not at work, what do you like doing?
Research, Blogging, playing football, Cooking...... the list goes on

What are your thoughts about The Guiding Voice platform?
It is a brilliant initiative. I love the drive with which you are trying to help people from various domains that play different roles. It gives clarity for the next phase of life, especially for students who are hungry for such guidance at the nascent stages of their careers.

Question to Self:
Are there any critiques or controversies surrounding the field I work in? If yes, will I step up to solve it? If not, can I come up with something innovative for the existing loopholes in it?

Tune into Suman's episode here:

13

Ignite Your Spirit: The Unyielding Journey of Vinoda Reddy.

She is a fitness enthusiast, motivator, and certified yoga teacher inspiring others on their wellness journey.

How many times you have decided to be on a fitness journey, maybe successfully started too, as a new year resolution. But failed at some point in time, maybe within a week's time or in a few months, if you are lucky!

We won't call it a 'failure' though! It is just that we all fail to stay consistent and committed to things for a longer period. And simply excuse us for doing so without any regrets!

But our perception towards commitment changed when we recorded this podcast episode with Vinoda Reddy - living proof that transformative power knows no boundaries.

In the heart of Telangana, India, Enugala Vinoda Reddy is a beacon of inspiration. A homemaker turned fitness enthusiast, whose awe-inspiring journey sets ablaze the hearts of thousands. Her story is a testament to the tenacity of the human spirit and a reminder that it's never too late to embark on a transformative fitness journey.

Vinoda's path to fitness began much later in life, challenging the notion that age is not a barrier to chasing our dreams. She took her first step towards a healthier lifestyle by practising yoga for two years, and although her dedication wavered when she joined the gym for another two years, her inner flame never extinguished. It was during this time that destiny intervened with an Instagram post by the renowned fitness expert and actress, Mandira Bedi[4]. The post captured her attention, sparking a life-changing decision.

On that fateful day, July 4th, 2020, Vinoda took the plunge, committing to a personal 365-day workout challenge. Little did she know that this would become the genesis of a thousand-day journey, reshaping not just her physique but also her entire perspective on life. As the days turned into weeks, and weeks into months, Vinoda accomplished her 1000-day challenge of fitness. Her journey inspired many others, especially homemakers who took similar challenges for various durations and are on their path to completing it. Her dedication grew stronger with this, as she now finds herself on her second 1000-day challenge.

Vinoda's approach to her fitness regime is as dynamic as her workouts. Embracing flexibility, she understands that true progress lies in adaptation and evolution. Managing multiple WhatsApp groups with over 3000 members, she became a guiding light, motivating and supporting others on their path to a healthier lifestyle. What unites this community is the weekly challenges, fostering a sense of togetherness in the pursuit of wellness.

The power of consistency is a mantra close to Vinoda's heart. However, her journey was not without

---

[4] *Mandira Bedi is an Indian actress, fashion designer,[2] and television presenter. She gained recognition by playing the titular role in the 1994 television show, Shanti, which was telecast on India's national channel, Doordarshan.*
https://en.wikipedia.org/wiki/Mandira_Bedi

challenges. Balancing her career, family responsibilities, and her own wellness was no easy feat. She didn't compromise on the daily needs of the family and her unwavering determination fuelled her resolve to carve out time for her fitness pursuits too. As she delved deeper into the world of yoga, she discovered its transformative power beyond the physical aspects—it nourished her mind, body, and soul.

Her wisdom reveals that:

Waiting for the perfect moment is futile; true transformation begins in the present.

Daily actions, regardless of their duration, yield remarkable results. Her journey exemplifies the potency of incremental progress, building confidence and resilience with each small achievement.

Her simplicity-driven philosophy dispels the myth that fitness and nutrition must be complex. Basic guidelines, like dedicating time to daily walks and nourishing our bodies with wholesome meals, lay the foundation for vibrant well-being. By embracing a balanced and sustainable approach, she shows that true health arises from self-love and care.

Vinoda's approach to her fitness regime is as flexible as the movements she embraces. Instead of being confined to rigid rules and a specific style, she understands that true progress lies in the ability to adapt and evolve. Not only this, but she also strongly believes that the path to building a good physique is with mental wellness.

Vinoda's belief in the profound connection between physical and mental fitness echoes in the words of co-author Naveen Samala. Naveen also started his fitness journey when he was 16 and ever since there has been no looking back. He makes sure that he works out an hour to 90 minutes on a normal day. If the situation doesn't permit or things are not so favourable, he at least exercises for 15 mins. Their shared journey spanning decades illuminates how pushing physical boundaries fortifies mental resilience. When we challenge ourselves physically, our minds grow stronger, propelling us to greatness in all aspects of life.

Follow your passion—this mantra lies at the core of Vinoda's journey.

With unwavering determination, she encourages us all to identify our deepest desires and embrace them wholeheartedly. Through practice and consistency, we unlock our true potential. Vinoda's unyielding commitment to discipline inspires others to weave it into the fabric of their lives.

And while Vinoda Reddy's journey is an invitation to fitness, it already extends a fiery glow to every reader's heart. It's a call to embrace transformative fitness journeys, regardless of age or circumstances. Her story ignites the spark within, reminding us that it's never too late to pursue our dreams and live a vibrant life. With unwavering passion and dedication, Vinoda has become a guiding voice for countless individuals, empowering them to unveil the incredible strength that lies within.

The time is now - let your fitness journey kindle the flame of inspiration for those around you.

Vinoda's journey as a fitness enthusiast and motivator had a ripple effect. Her influence extended to social media platforms, where she shared her experiences, tips, and motivational messages. Her digital presence became a source of inspiration for a global audience, touching lives across borders and cultures.

Physical fitness is not just about shaping the body; it's about nurturing the mind. A strong body empowers us to embrace life's challenges with unwavering confidence and mental wellness.

And before you jump onto scrolling her social media and taking that fitness resolution, here's a fun-filled rapid-fire round with Vinoda to inspire you a bit more with her life's anecdotes:

What is your favourite failure?
Nothing that I remember. Life has been fair to me so far.

What are the hardships you went through while going through your life/career journey?
I had my share of financial struggles during childhood.

What is your planned vs actual career path?
I have done an MBA and worked in the corporate world. But my passion lies in fitness, which I turned into my profession.

What is the turning point in your life?
To put it in a date- July 4, 2020- The day I have taken up 365 days challenge and that changed my life.

One person that influenced you the most & how?
Mandira Bedi: With her inspiration, I have started the 365-day workout challenge and that has changed my life.

Name one incident that transformed your life.
Doing Advanced Yoga Certification has transformed my life.

One thing you would do differently in the past?
I wish I could've started running a bit earlier.

Your Vision/Goal/ in life and what are you trying to achieve?
I want to influence and motivate people to live a healthy and active life.

What is the Craziest/Naughtiest thing you have done in childhood?
In my childhood, I got caught by my maths teacher when I manipulated my maths marks on paper. I had to change it because I failed.

What is the hidden/unknown/least known fact about you?

Everyone thinks I love cooking but that's actually what I hate the most. And people don't believe it when I say so.

What is your favourite fantasy gadget that you want for yourself/want to invent?
Want to invent a gadget which will automatically edit and upload all my workout-related videos on my Instagram page and YouTube.

If you are not at work, what do you like doing?
Listening to 90s music.

How do you keep yourself up to date? Please share links or references to websites/blogs/books etc.
Instagram and YouTube.

One piece of advice you want to give to the youngsters in the field.
Consistency is key; follow your passion.

What are your thoughts about The Guiding Voice platform?
The Guiding Voice is a blessing to me. It has changed my life, thank you so much.

Quote or Anecdote that you strongly believe in?
Something is better than nothing.

Tune into Vinoda's English Episode here:

14

Tribikram Rath: An Extraordinary Journey of an Entrepreneur.

Bhubaneshwar - It was in this unassuming place that a remarkable story began! A story that would propel a man named Tribikram Rath on an extraordinary journey of self-discovery, courage, and determination.

We all know at least one young entrepreneur around us. And we are so grateful for these entrepreneurs creating a difference in our lives every day with their innovative startups.

But while all the young entrepreneurs are soaring high with courage and determination to make things happen, some 40+ age entrepreneurs are jumping into entrepreneurship at the second innings of their careers. One such individual is TriBikram Rath or as he is known, Tri.

Tri started his career as a regular full-time employee at GE. He joined there as a project manager. Armed with a brilliant mind and an insatiable curiosity, Tribikram quickly made a name for himself within the organization. His exceptional technical expertise, coupled with his innovative thinking, propelled him up the ranks to become a Director in Quality Assurance Engineering. This earned him the trust and respect of his peers and superiors alike, although this didn't come easy to him.

Throughout his professional journey at GE, Tri proved himself to be a distinctive leader in the testing and quality assurance domain. He has vast experience in the areas of evaluation, implementation and developing customized test automation solutions using industry tools like Selenium, Perfecto Mobile, LoadRunner, Squish, Eggplant, Robotic Process Automation, UiPath, Jenkins, Cooley, script less tools like work soft Or Felicia QA inspect, Burp Suite, etc, covering test automation, performance engineering and application security testing. He has led quality assurance process maturity and transformation for complex projects to deliver lasting testing solutions to end customers. He also introduced touchless or continuous testing to support the DevOps ecosystem.

Tri also led and implemented ISO 9001 2000 controls and the Capability Maturity Model (CMM) for enterprises during his early career phase. Tri developed several dot-net and multimedia-based applications and authored technical publications and articles online.

"Software testing is a very good career option if you have a real passion to analyse software, apps or products to detect defects intelligently and ensure that software and products meet all their design criteria before they go to production." ~Tri Rath

According to Tri, if you aim at becoming an automation test engineer, then you must learn automation, knowledge of any scripting language like your VB script or JavaScript programming, language, like C++ or maybe some fundamentals of Java. Knowledge of a database or SQL queries, basic Linux commands tests and defect management tools will always help assure a better career in testing.

In his view, test engineers should learn the art or science of how to break the applications in more failure case scenarios. So, in that context, he recommends a book: *How to Break Web Software, a Practical Guide to Testing* by Mike Andrews and James Whitaker. This book is recommended for test engineers who are in the early career phase. That would enlighten them with certain new techniques on how to find defects that cannot be captured with normal automation scenarios. So, you have to be innovative to find those flaws, and this book talks about how to break web software.

Talking of soft skills, as a Software Automation Test Engineer, you need to have the right team spirit and should be comfortable working as a team. You need to help each other by focusing on the quality of the overall software, collaborating with other members, helping them be flexible to the needs of work, constantly learning new skills and techniques, and quickly accepting organizational changes.

As Tri's tenure with GE surpassed the two-decade mark, he found himself at crossroads. A deep longing to embark on a new adventure tugged at his heart. Fuelled by an entrepreneurial spirit, he made a momentous decision—to channel his vast experience, expertise, and life savings into founding his own technology company.

With a vision in mind and an unyielding determination, Tri set up the doors of his tech venture in the heart of Bhubaneswar - his hometown. The company is named Mohs10 Technologies, which means *'Strength of a diamond.'* His vision behind having this name is to reinforce to their clients that the solutions offered by his company are as strong as the Diamond. The company aims to focus on building the generation of cutting-edge capabilities around Software Testing, Software Quality Engineering and intelligent automation solutions by leveraging futuristic technologies like Artificial Intelligence and Machine Learning (AI/ML) etc. covering Functional, Performance and Security aspects of the enterprise applications from technology domains like Web, Mobile, Blockchain, IoT, OTT, AR/VR, AI, ERP & SAAS/Cloud.

It was a daring move that required Tri to navigate uncharted waters, as he ventured from the security of a corporate behemoth to the uncertain terrain of entrepreneurship.

Mohs10 Technologies quickly gained traction, attracting bright minds and talented individuals who shared Tri's passion for innovation. Together, they forged a culture of collaboration and relentless pursuit of excellence. The team is self-motivated and is always beaming with energy. They are passionate about solving customers' problems. You will see all the team members with a big smile on their faces and display an immense maturity level. Thanks to this team, the company's portfolio is now expanding rapidly. Tri's ability to combine his technical expertise with astute business acumen proved to be a winning formula. Tri is not only developing his venture, but he is also contributing to the growth and development of the startup ecosystem in Odisha. He is instrumental in organising tech conferences at Bhubaneshwar by inviting industry experts from across the country. And with strong support/partnership from the Government. His dream is to make Bhubaneshwar another destination for Tech talent.

Beyond the success of his company, Tri never forgot his roots. He recognised the power of technology to uplift underserved communities and empower the less fortunate. Through Mohs10 Technologies, he initiated several philanthropic projects, leveraging technology to bridge the digital divide and provide access to education in a Tier-2 city like Bhubaneswar.

Here's a quote that Tri most relates with-

Just the way our fingerprints are unique, the time each of us lives in is also 100% unique in terms of the environmental factors, the challenges we face, the opportunity we have and so on. Trust yourself and do it!

We are sure you agree with us when we say that the name Tribikram Rath is synonymous with a visionary leader, and a beacon of hope for the marginalized. His journey of creating a startup has touched the lives of countless individuals, igniting a spark within them and challenging the status quo.

But behind this CEO, is a fun-loving individual and a playful father. Here's an impromptu Rapid-Fire round we had with Tri.

What is the one cartoon character you can relate to?
Pink Panther.

What is the one rule you want to implement across India, if you get a chance?
I would like to eliminate bribes.

If you get a chance to be a hero in one of the movies, which movie remake would you like to work on?

I am an old-school fan of Amitabh Bachchan and would love to act in any of his old movies, like, Silsila and Kabhi-Kabhi.

What is the one dish you can eat for a lifetime?
We have a local dish in Bhubaneshwar, called Dalma - A mix of Dal and vegetables. It is thicker than Sambhar.

What is the one fantasy gadget you would like to invent?
My Daughter introduced me to this movie sequence from Interstellar, and that got me the idea to have a time instrument that should not let you age.

What is the one tip you have for the youth of India?
Get a Mentor in your life! A person who can guide you through the path and can also provide inputs by reviewing your present plan.

What is one of the craziest/Naughtiest things you have done in childhood?
Mimicking my dad and other elders in the neighbourhood to show the world how I will look and behave when I grow up, get married and have a family. I loved biology. Liked home gardening, experimented on plant grafting, and dissected live animals like frogs, cockroaches etc. to explore their internal organs.

Your Vision/Goal/ in life and what are you trying to achieve?
Our Indian scriptures have influenced me and my leadership skills a lot. I read 'Srimad Bhagavad Gita' almost every day. I strongly believe in 'Vasudhaiva Kutumbakam'! I want to contribute significantly to my

Matrubhoomi (India) and my Janmabhoomi (Bhubaneswar) through opportunity creation for our youth, social causes etc. for the rest of my career. MOHS10 turned 2 years old in August 20223 and we started generating some revenue. I have already created some goals for 2023 to initiate some CSR activities starting Q4 2023.

What are your thoughts about The Guiding Voice platform?

TGV is a very inspiring platform for professionals and entrepreneurs at all levels. It inspired me as well. You guys are working very hard to maintain consistency! All my best wishes and keep rocking TGV!

<table>
<tr><td>

Question to Self:
How can I leverage my skills and resources to empower the local community and generate employment opportunities?

</td></tr>
</table>

Tune into Tri's English Episode here:

15

Hemalatha Rao: An Unbreakable Spirit of Resilience

Her story is a beacon of hope, a reminder that no matter the odds stacked against us, we can emerge victorious.

If you have come reading this book so far, you would know that the pages in this book are about captivating and inspiring journeys we encounter in our day-to-day lives. And people who survive through adversity and win are no less than superheroes!

One such superwoman we came across is Hemalatha AKA, Hema. A woman whose life can be defined as no less than a warrior. Who won over the adversities just by smiling through in every situation.

Hema's journey of health issues started in her early childhood. At a tender age, she was diagnosed with Atrial Septal Defect (ASD), commonly known as 'a hole in the heart.' She faced a life-threatening situation as soon as she came into the world. But through a successful surgery, she defied fate and returned to what seemed like a normal life.

As she entered the eighth grade, breathlessness during physical activities became a constant companion. Revealing the persistence of her cardiac issues. She underwent a diagnosis, only to find out that she had pulmonary hypertension, a rare and debilitating condition. In more common terms, the relentless pressure in her lungs strained her heart, making even the simplest physical exertion a herculean task.
But Hema was not the one to surrender easily. She pressed on, completing her schooling, graduating, and even pursuing a PhD.

With each hurdle she faced, her determination only grew stronger. She was a living testament to the fact that adversity can either break you or mould you into something even stronger.

As soon as she finished her PhD, she decided to pursue her Master's Diploma in Software Engineering. And later secured a position at Sony India as a Software Engineer. Being in a career that involves commuting added stress to her life. This was a new thing for Hema to deal with. Her home-to-office commute involved 30kms of travel in Bengaluru (India) traffic. This took a toll on her health and medical experts suggested she be on external oxygen for a lifetime. But Hema was born to fight adversities! While she took precautions and listened to medical experts, she also got involved in yoga and acupressure. This gradually regained her lung strength and improved her overall condition.

Around the year 2000-2001, she took a significant leap and founded 'Horizon Placement'- an International Head-Hunting Firm that serves businesses by providing them with the right candidate that matches the role requirements. This venture came with its own set of challenges, particularly in candidate sourcing due to high demand and limited supply. But Hema's determination to win challenges is reflected here too! She kept moving forward and in 2002, the venture finally started making a profit.

Also on the personal front, she got married and defied the societal expectation of a perfect bride! Her husband wholeheartedly embraced her medical challenges. Their journey together involved seeking advanced medical treatments in the UK, where Hema faced yet another health battle in the form of Peripheral Neuropathy, an autoimmune disease.

Eventually, Hema found herself at a crossroads where a heart and lung transplant became her only viable option. The decision-making process and the subsequent counselling were arduous. But her positivity shone through like a beacon of hope, and she made a decision.

Hema attributes her success to three essential elements: maintaining a positive attitude, reframing negative thoughts into positive ones, and never giving up.

She firmly believes that for every problem, there is a solution waiting to be discovered. Additionally, she credits her success to divine intervention, unwavering family support, and the exceptional medical professionals who stood by her side.

Along with the never-giving-up attitude and thriving in her career, she made minor changes in her life to live through and make her medical challenges easier. To start with, she transitioned her workspace to the ground floor of her home. She focused on her strengths and managed her health smartly. Living abroad presented its own unique set of challenges, including the daily struggles of grocery shopping and dealing with her husband's health issues. But she managed that too with the support of the community and her family.

While Hema is one warrior we interacted with, the significance of health has been highlighted at the onset of COVID-19. And we all can't undermine it till today!

Today Hema is a staunch advocate for organ donation, tirelessly spreading awareness about its importance and its potential to change lives. She is actively engaged in support groups, extending her support and experience to those grappling with pulmonary hypertension and heart-lung transplants.

In the face of adversity, Hema imparts invaluable advice: Setbacks are not the end, but merely a turn in the road.

She emphasizes the need to respect one's body, mind, and purpose in life, urging individuals not to waste their lives in self-pity. She champions the significance of a strong and fearless mindset, encouraging all to face life head-on.

Hema's journey is an inspiration, a reminder for all of us to be always armed with determination, positivity, and belief. In her story, we find the strength to conquer our mountains, to keep moving forward, and to embrace life's challenges with open arms. We hope it does the same magic on you.

We have also uncovered some lightning-quick wisdom with Hema and got to know some insights that have fuelled her remarkable resilience. Read this rapid-fire round:

What is your favourite failure?
Failure to die.

**What was your planned career path vs the actual
one that happened?**
I planned to have a career in Biosciences. But I ended
up being in Software.

What is the turning point of your life?
Meeting Mr. Ian Faria and undergoing Heart and lung
transplant.

People who influenced you the most & how?
My Mother - by her strong willpower, and husband with
strong decision making.

One incident that transformed your life
When I met my Guru, Dr. Bannanje Govindaacharya
*(an Indian philosopher and Sanskrit scholar versed in
Veda Bhashya, Upanishad Bhashya, Mahabharata,
Puranas and Ramayana. He wrote Bhashyas on Veda
Suktas, Upanishads, ShataRudriya, Brahma Sutra
Bhashya, and Gita Bhashya and was an orator.)*

One thing you would do differently in the past.
Listen to the doctor and start my treatment for
neuropathy much earlier.

**Your Vision/Goal/ in life and what are you trying to
achieve?**
Motivate as many people as possible and instil
confidence in them.

Craziest/Naughtiest thing you have done in childhood.
I have bitten three people out of which one had to take an injection.

Favourite fantasy gadget that you want for yourself/want to invent.
Invent a gadget which will prevent all the bad radiation from reaching living entities.

If you are not at work, what do you like doing?
Watch movies.

How do you keep yourself up-to-date?
DD channels for world news, https://www.w3schools.com/ and Udemy.com for software-related courses. And of course, Google!

One piece of advice you want to give to the youngsters in the field.
Conviction and hard work are assured paths to success.

What are your thoughts about The Guiding Voice platform?
A very friendly platform with a novel cause of bringing amazing stories of unknown heroes.

Quote or Anecdote that you strongly believe in?
Inspire till you expire.

Tune into Hemalatha's episode here:

16

Tech Whisperer: Yashwant's Journey to Become an Influencer.

Yashwant is a tech alchemist who turned his dreams into a golden reality, inspiring others to follow their own paths.

Ed Catmull in his book *Creative Inc.* said, *"**Don't wait for things to be perfect before you share them with others. Show early and show often. It'll be pretty when we get there, but it won't be pretty along the way.**"*

And as we quote this, we recall the journey of the TGV. We started from a room to now have a brand-new studio with professional equipment. But this journey of years wasn't all sweet fruit. We learned along the way, and failed at times, just to get up and become better. But what sets us apart from others is that '**we started**'.

Find the courage to take that first step and trust yourself to figure things out as you keep walking.

Yashwant Sai Palaghat is a name you might have come across if you scroll YouTube for tech trends. If not, allow us to introduce you to this name. Yashwant is a tech enthusiast who has always been curious about the world of technology. The years of exposure to the internet and resources taught him the power of storytelling. He, being a techie, decided to merge the two and build an ecosystem of telling all the tech stories in the most creative way.

Yashwant's journey started in 2016 when he was a college student. While most of his friends were solely focused on their classroom courses, Yashwant started researching technology trends, participating in events, and getting onto social media to create content for college. He formed multiple clubs in college and was an extrovert who loved networking with peers. Spending time on the internet clicked him with an idea to create content, put it on YouTube and interact with a wider set of audience. In his early days as a content creator, Yashwant used to jot down his ideas on sticky notes and post them on his room wall. He wasn't an expert in content creation at first, but he was determined to learn and improve over time. Being a newbie in the field didn't discourage him; it only fuelled his passion.

As the years passed, Yashwant mastered digital marketing and content creation. He learnt by sharing and failing and understanding the importance of audience interaction with content. He already knew how to effectively communicate complex tech concepts and eventually learned Digital Marketing. Yashwant's secret was- *his commitment*. He spent around 2-3 hours a day keeping up with market trends, ensuring his content was always relevant.

Yashwant became an influential content creator, digital marketing manager, and author by 2020, the year of the COVID-19 pandemic. Like many others, Yashwant found himself with more time on his hands due to lockdowns and restrictions. Instead of letting this time go to waste, he decided to explore his passion for technology and content creation. He followed other content creators and refined his art of storytelling. Knowing Tech, he also started creating programming courses on Udemy, sharing his knowledge with others who were eager to learn. His enthusiasm for teaching was evident in every lesson he crafted, and it didn't take long for his courses to gain popularity.

In 2022, Yashwant took a leap of faith and wrote his first book, '***Door to Financial Freedom***.' The book was a reflection of his personal journey and the lessons he had learned along the way. Yashwant wanted to inspire others to unleash their potential and achieve financial freedom, just as he had.

Yashwant lives by the Mantra of –
"Consistency, fresh ideas, and updated content."

He knows that to stand out in the noisy world of social media, these are the principles to live by!

But as easy as it sounds, Creative blocks, even for Yashwant, are inevitable. To deal with those, he has a strategy- on some days, he would create multiple pieces of content, and on others, he'd take a break to recharge his creativity. It is this balance that kept his ideas fresh and innovative.

Yashwant had a piece of advice he would often share with aspiring content creators – "Don't focus on monetizing your content; focus on sharing knowledge and adding value."

He dedicates his workdays to his professional responsibilities and personal projects, leaving his weekends free for relaxation and spending time with loved ones. For him, creating content is not just a job; it is his passion. The brainstorming process excites him, and he puts his heart and soul into every piece he creates. He knows the importance of consuming content and is picky about who he follows and learns from.

Yashwant Sai Palaghat's story is a testament to what one can achieve through passion, dedication, and a genuine desire to help others. He inspires countless individuals to follow their dreams, unleash their potential, and achieve financial freedom. Yashwant's journey serves as a reminder that when you love what you do and share your knowledge with the world, the possibilities are endless.

As we leave you with a thought to follow your passion and how you can shape it, read quick and unfiltered insights we have from Yashwant's life through this rapid-fire round:

What is your favourite failure?
I couldn't make it to IIT after my 12th. It's my favourite because it helped me to face challenges and to become stronger.

What are some hardships in your life/career journey?
Having graduated from a tier-3 college, I faced many problems including limited opportunities, a network with less interest in careers & no real external motivation to take risks. I told myself to cross all of them by thinking and doing things out of the routine.

What is your planned vs actual career path?
I planned to become a programming geek in my earlier days & later developed an interest towards creativity & content creation. I am currently working in a full-time job as a Digital Marketing Manager & a part-time content creator.

What is the turning point in your life?
The day I started creating content & sharing knowledge.
It helped me realise my strengths.

What is one incident that transformed your life?
During my college days, I attended numerous
competitions across the country and bagged many
awards which pushed me to explore new opportunities.

**What is your Vision/Goal/ in life and what are you
trying to achieve?**
To become a full-time content creator and transform the
way people learn things (at least a 0.0001%
contribution towards it)

What is one least known fact about you?
Not everyone in my network knows about it but I am a
huge cricket/movie fan. I watch everything.

**If you are not at work or creating content, what do
you like doing?**
Watching movies and travelling.

**One piece of advice you want to give to the
youngsters in the field.**
Explore as many careers as you can during your 20s.
The 20s are to experiment but not to settle.

**What are your thoughts about The Guiding Voice
platform?**
One of the great initiatives, and it's very close to my
ideology towards career development.

Quote or Anecdote that you strongly believe in? (It may be your quote or something that resonated with you)
Never put 100% into one thing (Job, Academics, Hustle), there is a life beyond it.

<table><tr><td>

Question to Self:
How can I harness my skills and knowledge to educate the world and make a positive impact on others?

</td></tr></table>

Tune into Yaswant's English Episode here:

17

Omita Gaikwad: Embracing Serenity Through Adversity.

From battling cancer to navigating the complexities of single parenthood, Omita's life story is woven with courage, and unyielding determination.

How do we see life?

For most of us, it is a blend of joy, sorrow, triumphs and setbacks - to put it in the easiest terms. Omita Gaikwad is no different! Her journey stands as a testament to the resilience of the human spirit, the power of self-awareness, and the transformational magic that emerges from the depths of adversity.

As Omita embarked on her voyage through life, she encountered more than her fair share of challenges. To start with, she faced the harrowing ordeal of cancer not once, but twice, navigating through illness and recovery. She experienced the painful dissolution of a marriage, taking on the role of a single parent to her daughter. All this grappled with anxiety, debt, and burnout while carrying the weight of managerial and leadership roles. Her story is not one of losing it to the darkness, but of rising above it with unyielding determination.

When we got to know about Omita's journey, we were left speechless. With several questions in mind, we approached her to learn about the journey. Her first statement was, "I am incredibly blessed and fortunate" to live through all and thrive.

She was diagnosed with cancer first at the age of 21. It was cured then and relapsed after 20 years amid the pandemic. She had thyroid cancer, which is in the neck area of the body. So, every time there is a sort of surgery around the neck, and dissections are made, there's a huge risk. It comes with excessive bleeding and a risk of losing your voice.

The second time it happened, she was a single mother to a 14-year-old. Her only concern then was to take care of her child and beat this for her. *Salute to Motherhood!* She equipped herself with certain knowledge tools and techniques which enabled her to respond to her recurrence. Her thought process became more positive. Her most recent surgery was in October 2021 when the Covid pandemic was pretty much in full force. It was a really big operation and she had to leave her daughter alone for the first time. Since the family was in a different city, they both made a conscious decision to grow through the situation and not give in.

The accessibility to medical facilities and being able to have her daughter's support reminded Omita to have even more gratitude towards life.

Through the haze of these trials, Omita's strength and positivity shine brighter than ever. Facing the unknown, she remained grounded, focused on the present moment. She found her guiding light—self-awareness and personal transformation. She discovered that within the depths of adversity lies the potential for boundless growth, profound happiness, and limitless personal power. Her story is a testament to the fact that challenges, when met with the right mindset and tools, can become steppingstones to greatness.

Her advice to others in distress echoes with wisdom: Keep doing what you're doing to stay positive. Embrace each day as a gift, unwrap its possibilities, and revel in the richness of experiences.

Uplifting, empowering, and enabling others to transform their lives and businesses became Omita's mission—a mission that breathed life into her very being. Armed with an unquenchable thirst for knowledge and personal evolution, she embarked on her everlasting PhD from the University of Life. She fortified herself with certifications in Neuro-Linguistic Programming, Performance and Happiness life coaching, Stress Management, Clinical and Naturopathic Nutrition, and Yoga. These tools formed the foundation upon which she built her core focus: WELLBEING, MINDSET, and PURPOSE.

Guided by her journey and armed with a repertoire of transformational tools and techniques, Omita helps her clients transition from states of exhaustion to resiliency, from confusion to clarity, and from overwhelm to ease. She empowered them to navigate life's storms with grace and fortitude, tapping into an endless flow of positive energy and intuitive abilities. Through her guidance, they become architects of their success, enhancing performance, productivity, and authenticity.

Omita's presence in the world is nothing short of extraordinary. A beacon of personal transformation, she ignites well-being and oneness, guiding others to embrace their true potential and find happiness. Her message resonates deeply, particularly in times of global turmoil such as the Covid-19 pandemic. Stress surged into lives worldwide, leaving many anxious, fatigued, and uncertain. Omita's voice emerged as a soothing balm, reminding us that amidst hardships, transformation is possible.

In Omita's story, we find the inspiration to navigate our adversities with grace, emerge stronger, and create a life that radiates with serenity and purpose.

Let's dive into a rapid-fire round, capturing swift insights from Omita about pivotal moments in her remarkable journey.

What is your favourite failure?
I don't believe there is anything such as failure, as life is an endless journey of learning and expansion

What are some of the hardships you went through while going through life/career journey?
Racism, cancer twice, divorce, single parenthood, burnout, cultural exclusion, anxiety and debt

What is one major turning point in your life?
Burnout and debt - never wanted to experience that again so gained much-needed clarity and momentum through that experience.

Who is one person that influenced you the most and how?
My father - both intentionally and unintentionally. His life's journey and hardships along with his teachings and preachings inspired me and created a very resilient core and instilled a humble love and appreciation for the gift of life. Simultaneously, his methods of teaching and preaching in my opinion were not so enabling and created much contrast within me which in turn inspired clarity and a desire to discover WHO I was and WHY I was here.

What is one incident that transformed your life?
Birth of my daughter - having experienced thyroid cancer for the first time at the young age of 21, there was a possibility that my health condition would affect my ability to conceive and have a healthy child. I miscarried and then went through a traumatic and challenging pregnancy. I was having a tough time in my marriage with my husband and in-laws, but my daughter was miraculously born. She was the brightest light in my life and inspired me to choose happiness for myself. For a child to know happiness the mother/parent needs to share this through their joy - I began my journey of self-discovery through and with my precious daughter.

What is one thing you would do differently in the past?
To be honest, Nothing! I would not be who I am today without the exact experiences that I had, and I love life and who I am in this, here and now.

What is your Vision/Goal/ in life and what are you trying to achieve?
I am not trying to achieve anything - each day I simply aspire to BE, fully, freely and fearlessly who I AM

What is the hidden/unknown/least known fact about you?
I act more like a 4-year-old than a 45-year-old most of the time.

If you are not at work, what do you like doing?
I love walking, listening to music, cooking, reading, doing yoga and meditation.

How do you keep yourself up to date?
I believe time is a mental construct. So, I don't focus on 'keeping up to date' - I am an intuitively led individual and allow nature's rhythm and timing to align me with whatever information I need at any given moment in time. Google has had a big role to play in this.

What are your thoughts about The Guiding Voice platform?
You are significant and enough.

One piece of advice you want to give to the youngsters in the field.
Raw, inspiring, enabling and a blessing to so many.

<table>
<tr><td>Question to Self:
What are three things I am genuinely grateful for in my life right now?</td></tr>
</table>

Tune into Omita's Episode here:

18

The Power of Storytelling:
Sourish Ghosh's Journey.

*Through stories, we become not just
tellers but also listeners, voyaging into
the realms of imagination, empathy, and
understanding.*

Storytelling is a timeless art, an age-old tradition woven into the fabric of human existence. Be it the regional folklore, ancient scripts or books! It's a power that transcends cultures, languages, and generations. At its core, storytelling is a profound act of connection, a way for us to share our experiences, dreams, and wisdom with one another. They can heal wounds, bridge divides and ignite the flames of change. This is the story of one such storyteller - Sourish Ghosh; who explored the magical world of storytelling to harness its power and decided to illuminate our lives with his inspiring journey.

In a world filled with data and technology, where communication is often reduced to bullet points and PowerPoint presentations, Sourish has spent the past two decades championing the timeless art of storytelling. At present, he is a transformational storyteller and coach. But his journey into the world of storytelling was not merely a career choice. It was a calling rooted in his upbringing.

Hailing from the vibrant city of Kolkata, he was raised in a household where storytelling was not just an art; it was a way of life. His parents, ardent storytellers themselves, exposed him to the intricate weave of Indian mythology. where heroes like Ram, Arjuna, and Krishna came alive through the narratives passed down through generations. It was in this environment that Sourish imbibed the stories of both the virtuous and the flawed, learning valuable life lessons from each.
One vivid memory from his childhood is the celebration of Durga Puja during Dussehra. It was a time when the goddess Durga was not merely a deity but a character in a grand epic – the Ramayana. When his Dad

narrated this story to him, he realised that storytelling could transcend time and space, connecting people across generations and cultures.

And that was just a start! Until this time, Sourish didn't think of making this a career choice. He just was in love with the stories his parents told him about various subjects. He decided to pursue his graduation and then post-graduation from a reputed college. However, in his post-grad, he was given the task of presenting to high-level corporate executives who had little patience for PowerPoint slides. It is at that moment he realised that he is a "brick and mortar" guy in a world rapidly digitizing. He has always believed in the power of human connection over technology. To engage these decision-makers on a personal level, he turned to the art of storytelling. Regardless of their corporate titles, these leaders were, first and foremost, human beings with emotions, aspirations, and experiences.

Stories allowed Sourish to tap into the world of storytelling as a career option and he decided to leave his MBA in just 9 months. Sourish started to train corporate employees in storytelling to better sell their products. We are sure at this point, you must be wondering what makes business storytelling unique. As Sourish put it: it's about infusing personal passion into one's work. He believes that anyone can become a storyteller, weaving their interests and passions into their professional life. The challenge lies in creating a compelling narrative in limited time with limited resources – a task that Sourish thrives on.

His formula for great storytelling is simple but profound:

***A great storyteller must also be a great listener,
attuned to the audience's reactions and emotions.***

One must either be living the story they tell or be
surrounded by a wealth of experiences.

Sourish's journey took an unexpected turn when he
hosted teachers from Norway and Sweden, who came
to India to learn storytelling and wished to introduce it
into their school curriculum. One of them expressed
admiration for India's culture, deeply rooted in stories.
This encounter made Sourish realize that the world
looked at India as a beacon of storytelling and culture.

Feeling a sense of responsibility, Sourish decided to
take his mission beyond corporate boardrooms. He
envisioned a world where every Indian, young and old,
embraced storytelling as a way of life, enriching our
culture and preserving our traditions for generations to
come.

But all said and done, while Sourish was making his
mark on the world with this skill set, a tragedy was
waiting for him. In 2021, Sourish faced a formidable
challenge - a sudden brain stroke that disrupted his life.
But instead of succumbing to this adversity, he saw it
as a divine signal to slow down and reflect. He
gradually got back on his toes and in the field of
storytelling with the help of his Doctors, Speech
Therapists, loved ones and the strong ecosystem he
has built in the past few years. Despite the lingering

effects of his health setback, Sourish's commitment to the art of storytelling remains unshaken.

Sourish's journey is a testament to the power of stories. His dedication to preserving the art of storytelling, his belief in its ability to bridge cultures and connect people, and his resilience in the face of adversity are a source of inspiration for all. In a world driven by technology, we can all take a moment to learn from Sourish's wisdom:

"The most potent tool for communication is not in our devices but in the stories we tell and the connections we forge."

And now gear up for a rapid-fire journey through the thoughts and insights of Sourish Ghosh:

What is your favourite failure?
My favourite failure in life would have been the inability to say no. I learned very late in life the importance of speaking my mind and not saying yes when I wanted to say no. As a result, I ended up doing things for others at the expense of my time and opportunity.

Beyond the Brain Stroke you went through, what are some of the other hardships you went through while going through your life/career journey?
Despite the difficulties—which may have been too numerous to count—I believe I emerged from them a stronger person.
An empty stomach taught me compassion and gratitude.

Working late nights taught me the essence of integrity and honour.

Waiting at a client's place, often for hours, taught me patience and the importance of time,

Being tired taught me the importance of hard work and a smile.

After my brain stroke, while lying paralyzed in bed with a tube through my nose to be fed, it taught me that I was not as alone in life and that when you work for others without malice, goodness comes back in multiples. It taught me to have faith in myself, appreciate the smaller things in life, and value the relationships around me.

I always remember these two dialogues from George Clooney's Up in the Air, where Clooney's character Ryan Birgham asks BOB, played by J.K. Simmons,
Ryan Birgham: "How much did they pay you to give up on your dreams?"
Bob: Twenty-seven thousand a year.
Ryan Bingham: "At what point were you going to stop and go back to what made you happy?" I'm not a shrink, I'm a wakeup call. I see guys who work at the same company their entire lives; guys exactly like you. They clock in and clock out, and they never have a moment of happiness. You have an opportunity; this is a rebirth; if not for you, do it for your children.

I believe that it's important to believe in yourself and to know your strengths and your happiness.

What is your plan vs the actual career path you chose?
My planned career was in Sales and Marketing, my actual career path is now that of a Storyteller, Writer, Coach and People Enhancer.

What is the turning point in your life?
It was when I had a brain stroke and lost all my abilities to speak, eat, swallow, walk, see, and move. The journey from there towards becoming fit once again and learning to walk, eat, swallow, laugh, cry, and work has been an uphill climb that has tested my belief in myself. I was a storyteller and writer who now could no longer speak, eat, write, draw, or travel. Being left to fend for myself during these testing times also taught me the importance of self-reliance and smile, which now I can, as my face slowly recovers from paralysis.

One person that influenced you the most & how?
My father has been the most influential person in my life. He passed away in the year 2000, but his teaching and words continue to guide me and urge me to get back on my feet and conquer the world. He was an avid storyteller himself, and from him, I got my interest in mythology, spirituality, science, and movies. He was an entrepreneur, and that mindset is what has shaped my career and decisions so far.

What is your Vision/Goal/ in life and what are you trying to achieve?
My vision in life is now to tell the stories of cultures and help transform the world through this. What I'm trying to achieve is to get my country, India, back to the level of world-class storytelling and culture it once revered.

Myopically I would love to tell stories on a world stage
like say TED TALKS, write a Book and travel the world
telling people stories and meeting new stories in life

**What is the Craziest/Naughtiest thing you have
done in childhood?**

As a child, I couldn't afford a ticket to see The Lion King
in a theatre. So, I called the theatre and tried to
convince them that seeing the film was essential. I
would have been 10 Yrs. then, and I didn't even know
whom I was talking to. It turned out that the person was
a curator at the cinema hall. He was impressed by my
dare and from then on, I always had three tickets
reserved for: me, my father and my sister. That was
another incident that made me develop a love for
movies and stories.

This incident ingrained in me the ability to speak my
mind and ask. It helped me interview stalwarts like Dr.
Mrs. Kiran Mazumdar Shaw, Mr. Nandan Nilekani,
Barkha Datt, Mr. Girish Karnad, author Chetan Bhagat,
Magician P C Sircar Junior, Mr. Ruskin Bond, Lord
Jeffrey Archer to name a few.

To think of it, it all started with the curator of Nandan in
Calcutta, believing the words of a 10 yr. old and his love
for movies and deciding to take a chance of admission
with him.

**Favourite fantasy gadget that you want for
yourself/want to invent.**

A dream recorder, with the ability to capture, record,
and replay dreams in full Technicolor. I often get vivid
dreams and find my ideas generated therein, but I am
at the mercy of my memory to recall these dreams.

How do you keep yourself up-to-date? Please share links or references to websites/blogs/books etc.
The Audible App, soundcloud.com, Spotify App, https://www.theguidingvoice.net/

One piece of advice you want to give to the youngsters in the field.
Never say no to opportunities. Say 'Yes' to that and then learn how to do so.

What are your thoughts about The Guiding Voice platform?
Amazing, poignant, relatable, reliable, fantastic, intriguing and exhaustive

One quote or anecdote that you strongly believe in?
My English teacher, Mrs K Goswami had once said to me, "*Sourish, Respect the chair a person sits on, if not the person.*"
This piece of advice has not only resonated with me but profoundly impacted and guided me since.

> ***Question to Self:***
> Q. What unique stories from my life can I share to connect with others and be a source of inspiration for someone?

Tune into Sourish's Episode here:

19

Vijay K Banda: 25 Years of Leadership and Innovation

What does it look like to have two and a half decades of diverse corporate experience? Is there any strategic expertise for success?

What does it strike you when we say an individual has 25 years of corporate experience? We assume it is - a boring 9-5 job! Or a tiring life of chasing money!

And though we agree with your version of corporate life, this isn't the case with everyone. Some we know are creating a fortune here with their enthusiasm and excitement to learn. If you can relate to this, you know what we are talking about. And if you can't, we have a word for you - CURIOSITY! A word that differentiates leaders from the rest of the crowd.

To have an affirmation of the thought process and be a guiding voice in your life, we happened to talk to Vijay K Banda, a seasoned IT professional with over 25 years of rich, insightful experience in the industry. Half of us reading this book are part of this corporate world in some or the other role. And a part of us feels a bit lost at times being in corporate and desire more. Vijay is one individual, who has been in this corporate world for 25 years and over time, created such a strong profile that he is now a go-to person for career planning and mentorship. Above all, a person who enjoys this journey of being.

Vijay has had a progressive career in information technology, working with various Fortune 500 companies across the globe in government, state healthcare, auto, pharmaceutical, telecom, and retail verticals - delivering end-to-end solutions. He carries an in-depth knowledge of security, cloud, and Oracle technologies, and most importantly, the ITSM framework. Beyond this, he is also an author, mentor, and speaker, with a proven track record of success in driving innovation, growth, and success for his clients and employers.

Now that you are familiar with Vijay and his portfolio of the steps to success, here's an interesting background to his story. Vijay's journey to success did involve a lot of wrong decisions and failures. But for 25 years, he still thrived every day to make things happen in his favour. One of his favourite failures is investing in the Electric Vehicle 2-wheeler business in 2005. He made a bold step when the market was not EV-ready. He tried for 5 years to penetrate and get a waiver for Sales Tax to have a competitive market price too but had no luck. We are sure, had it been done today he would have had better traction.

How does he count this as a steppingstone to his success?
"Pioneers may not be Entrepreneurs", which means sometimes going too early to the market can also lead to failure.

We are fortunate today to have mentors who guide us for a better entry into the market by analysing the product market fit.

We want to ask you at this moment - What was your favourite failure? And what was the lesson you have learnt from it?

And while you take a pause thinking about it, here is how Vijay summarises his attitude towards work and success in 4 Cs:

Curiosity: Vijay upholds curiosity above everything and gives it a major credit for succeeding at anything in life. We truly can't agree more with this! Curiosity led us to start this podcast and cater for a wider audience with this book.

For every college student and every IT professional, curiosity to learn and take challenging roles is the only way forward. Start not only by expanding your depth of technical competency but also, the breadth of IT. Because the future demands comb-shaped skills; Just like a comb has multiple verticals, you also have one horizontal with multiple verticals of talent under it. Stay agile and have a holistic 360-degree awareness of things.

Creativity: *When was the last time you ran into a problem and gave up on it before finding a workable solution?* There is always another way to look at things and all it takes is a little creative thought process to make things happen. The only condition is to stay persistent towards solving a problem and seek help when it is needed. Inculcating divergent thinking can also help in finding creative, simple but effective solutions which nobody else thought through

Collaboration: A team of individuals with different approaches to a problem can build a masterpiece. And maybe that's why Brainstorming sessions are always longer than the actual field work because more than half the battle has been won in the meeting room itself. We recommend you collaborate when needed, to bring a diverse set of thoughts to the table.

Credit: While the other three are what you should do, this one is a big no for doing! Do Not Chase Credits! Your best work is done and displayed when you do not seek credit or reward for it. Do not focus on the reward but put all your efforts in and enjoy the journey of making it happen. If you do not worry about who is going to get the credit in a team environment, you can create wonders as you all are aligned on a common goal of solving a problem.

Can we just take the liberty to tell you all how much we resonate with Vijay's thought process? Just like how we decided to write this book to guide the young ones for a better future, Vijay came up with a book on Skill Up India. The book talks about 4 Mantras which when recited and repeated every day will make you ready for the future. Here is a sneak peek at these 4 Mantras:

1. Develop Industry Awareness
2. Develop Self-Awareness
3. Adapt and Upskill
4. Attitude to Adapt

Vijay's intent behind writing the book was to guide the younger generation to have the right mindset and adapt to the pace of technology and changes in the world to be future-ready. The fact how education alone won't necessarily guarantee success in the long run and it is one's passion and qualifications that truly make a difference. With the rise of AI and automation, it is becoming even more necessary to develop skills that enable individuals to excel at the creative end of the spectrum. In a world where machines can perform routine tasks, it is the ability to think critically, solve problems, and come up with innovative solutions that will set individuals apart.

While a degree or diploma may provide a foundation of knowledge, it is the passion to learn and apply that knowledge that will make a difference.

Furthermore, individuals who have a deep-rooted passion for their field of work are more likely to stay motivated and pursue excellence throughout their careers, continuously learning and improving their skills. While education is vital, it is equally important to recognize the value of passion and qualifications in achieving long-term success, especially in an era where AI and automation are changing the way we work.

Vijay's episode was recorded in 2021. At the time of writing this book, ChatGPT4 was launched amidst the wave of AI automation across industries. Generating a lot of excitement and so many worries. The CXO community is much more excited about this technology than any other technology in the past. The pace at which we are seeing the progress of AI, especially generative AI, and the velocity at which companies are releasing products will have a compounding effect that we have never dealt with. This new AI revolution is creating panic among the young techies and job aspirants that their jobs will be taken away. But the workaround is to be adaptable by embracing AI tools. Learn how to use them, and find out use cases, which require complementary skills that only humans have. Voila! Your job is safe.

Having this conversation with Vijay on things beyond Academic Degrees and working on skill sets made this one of our favourite episodes. After all, Passion and developing qualifications made us start this podcast 3 years back and then progress to write this second volume of the book (**TGV Inspiring Lives**).

Vijay's Success Mantra is,
"There is no single silver bullet or silver lining to successful careers. Everybody has to create their career web. It's not a career path. You need to knit your career web and that is the success mantra."

Did we give you food for thought through this chapter?

While you are at it, put a pause to your thoughts for a while, because we are taking you on a candid rapid-fire round with Vijay:

What is the Craziest/Naughtiest thing you have done in childhood?
Taking long bicycle rides between schools

What are the hidden/unknown/least known facts about you?
I am a good dancer too.

What's your favourite fantasy gadget that you want for yourself/want to invent?
A Gratitude reminder that I can use every day.

If you are not at work, what do you like doing?
These days, it is Writing for me. Previously, I was into sports and loved playing cricket in my free time.

How do you keep yourself up to date? Please share links or references to websites/blogs/books etc.
Yesmentor.org. Also, I keep writing blogs and updating my book.

One piece of advice you want to give to the youngsters in the field.
You need to read my book for this. But if I have to put it out in one line-
Have a right and balanced definition of success for yourself.

Question to Self:
What specific skills do I want to acquire and how can I develop them? By asking yourself this question and actively pursuing the development of your desired skill set, you can position yourself for success in your chosen career path.

Tune into Vijay's English Episode here:

20

Dipika Trehan: A Journey of Purpose.

Let's unveil the enigma, where women silently struggle for an identity.

Look at the women around you - could be your mother, sister or wife! Do you see women shouldered with invisible burdens? While silently bearing responsibilities? Ever thought about where these burdens reap in? Maybe these are the societal biases and stereotypes that complicate their journey of life. And over the years of existence, being someone's Mother or wife is all they are identified with, which overshadows their years of hard work. And in this situation, it is not wrong to say that self-doubt creeps in as they grapple with imposter syndrome over time.

If this sounds sad to you, then you must know that it is the story of the majority of the women in the world. And Dipika's journey is one such tale. Except she decided to break this pattern and write her own story of empowerment and compassion. She's more than a leader; she's a trailblazer. As the founder and CEO of Corporate Diva, her mission transcends mere checkboxes for diversity, extending to a profound commitment to crafting an inclusive and equitable world for all.

Born into an Armed Forces family and later married to a military man, Dipika's life was marked by service from the very beginning. With an MBA in HR and training, she embarked on a corporate career spanning nearly a decade. However, life's ever-evolving circle led her to different countries for nearly a decade. But, ultimately, she returned to India and the corporate space she knew.

If anything, she has learnt from her global exposure and interactions with diverse individuals that – her life had a more profound purpose than the nine-to-five grind.

Dipika went to Israel, sponsored by the government of Israel, for a conference where women leaders from 23 countries were present. It is there she realised and got exposed to the biases and stereotypes women face across countries. With maternity being one of their biggest challenges. Feminine elements that women bring to work are perceived as weaknesses rather than strengths. As Dipika puts it, the two factors that every woman is hungry for are dignity and respect for the labour that they bring to the table.

At the same conference, Dipika met a Georgian lady who was a single child to her parents and the one thing she wanted in life was to have a nice big, happy family. So now she has 5 kids. But every time she conceived and delivered, she was questioned about her next big project, though she was simultaneously working on her PhD.

She's now an authority in Georgia, but even at this stage, she struggles every day with workplace bias. She is often asked- "How are you going to balance work along with 5 children"?

Though it is just one story of a woman, each of them at some point faced this. And it is common across the globe. What people need to realize is that a woman comes with multitasking skills, far better than the male gender. We can task our priorities well and perform effectively.

This epiphany and realisation led her to Bengaluru, a place where her journey towards becoming an empowered woman truly began. She made it a mission- to nurture women leaders until gender ceased to be a specification, and leadership flourished universally. Today, she is a 'philantropreneur' fuelled by unwavering passion.

She credits her journey to timely understanding and three pillars of success-

"Sabr" (Patience), "Shukr" (Gratitude), and "Samarpit" (Surrender)

Life presents challenges and knocks us down, but with **Patience**, we can trust the process.

Gratitude, not just for rewards, but for the lessons within setbacks, propels us forward.

Surrendering to a higher power when efforts seem fruitless can guide us to the right path.

The co-author of this book, Naveen Samala, resonates with the same belief as Dipika. He believes in the power of evolving to create a larger impact and hence started TGV (The Guiding Voice) in Telugu and Hindi languages.

However, this path to create a global impact was not a cakewalk for Dipika. She had to struggle to deal with the stereotypes in setting up the organization and getting women out of their comfort zones to seek more from life. It is over time that women believed in her purpose of '**Corporate Diva'** and she started shouldering responsibilities to them silently to make them feel more empowered.

But Dipika's share of troubles is not limited to this. As the organization was growing and she conceived, her maternity came with its own backlash. Less from the organization and much more from her own anxiety. Self-doubt crept in as she grappled with imposter syndrome.

Dipika overcame this by creating awareness about what women are capable of and can achieve. Dipika firmly believes in the distinctions between male and female leadership. Women bring empathy, compassion, and strong task-management skills to the table. These qualities have often been overlooked or misperceived as weaknesses. Women's community-driven nature fosters inclusive leadership that benefits organizations and nations.

Dipika's ultimate challenge was the absence of a professional sisterhood ecosystem. This void inspired her to create Corporate Diva, empowering women to carve their paths and earn the recognition they deserve. With this, she envisioned a system capable of quantifying women's worth and credibility. Such that it could accelerate progress toward gender equity, bridging the gap within her lifetime.

Her message to women is clear: "***Be authentic and vulnerable, dispelling the facade of perpetual strength. Expressing vulnerability and seeking*** *support not only helps women but may also inspire others to do the same."*

The barriers to women's leadership are often rooted in a lack of clarity in goals and a reluctance to voice their needs. Women must learn to communicate their objectives clearly and seek mentorship and support.

One of the women's remarkable assets is their ability to multitask effectively without compromising efficiency, setting them apart as effective leaders.

In the face of adversity, Dipika's journey stands as a testament to what can be achieved with patience, gratitude, and unwavering self-belief. Her dedication to empowering women and fostering inclusive leadership serves as a beacon of hope for gender balance in the professional world.

Through her story, we want the reader to embark on their journeys, embrace their authenticity, and overcome obstacles, knowing that the path to success is paved with resilience and purpose.

With the inspiring journey of Dipika Trehan laid out before us, let us now transition into a rapid-fire round where we delve into some quick insights and valuable takeaways from her remarkable story:

What is your favourite failure?
Moving countries and unknowingly moving into sabbatical, for what life had in store to teach, no job, no university, no cubicle could!

What are the hardships you went through while going through your life/career journey?
Lack of self-identity, lack of financial independence, lack of support system, lack of a mentor. My co-founder backstabbed me and took away a lot of my work. It made me learn that "*You can take the honey away from the bee, but you can never take away from her the craft of making honey.*" I was duped with a large amount of money because I was naive to trust someone on their verbal promises and gave little importance to legal paperwork. I learnt to be on top of contracts and MOUs. My clients would change the planned and approved budgets, with no prior notice and no compensation for the loss incurred at my end. My learning here was to have structured payment terms and compensation clauses for inconveniences. I was shown the door when I would speak about Corporate Diva incorporates, who perceived it as a ramp walk. I had the same clients years later come back to me to curate women leadership initiatives, with a brand value of Corporate Diva.

What is the major turning point in your life?
Taking that one decision to not give into the boxed perception of the term DIVA and continuing with conviction on my belief that 'Diva' is a feeling, a mindset and has almost nothing to do with physical appearance. It is intellect that excites me!

One person that influenced you the most & HOW?
There have been so many people who have crossed my path, and from each of them, I've learned. But It's my life journey and the way I navigate it that inspires me the most!

What is one incident that transformed your life?
The day I realised that instead of prioritising the world, I should prioritise myself. I slowly climbed the ladder in my priority list, and it has transformed me as an individual.

What is one thing you would do differently in the past?
I am a product of my journey. So, I would not want to change anything from my past, present or future.

What is your Vision/Goal/ in life and what are you trying to achieve?
My vision is simple: To live, breathe and thrive in an equal world. A world sans judgement, sans biases sans prejudices. And to get there, we need to bridge gender gaps. I am trying to do this via Corporate Diva and by being humane!

What is the craziest/naughtiest thing you have done in childhood?
Why only in childhood? I continue doing crazy things even today. As somewhere in the corner of my heart, I keep the child in me ALIVE!

What is one hidden/unknown/least known fact about you?
While I come across as an extrovert and fun-loving person, I am a deep soul who is very sceptical about humour. As sometimes words said jokingly scar someone for life.

What is your favourite fantasy gadget that you want for yourself/want to invent?
A gadget that speaks for a woman's worth and her credibility, because she thinks there is still time for Women to speak up for themselves.
As per the World Economic Forum, we're still 99.5 years away from gender equity and equality. So if there's a gadget that can speak our worth and communicate that and put that worth into action for a fast-paced closing of the gender gap uh and especially if it can be done within the timeline line that- She is alive.

If you are not at work, what do you like doing?
I like spending time with myself, in silence. Other times, I listen to music and sing.

One piece of advice you want to give to the youngsters in the field.
Trust your gut and never, ever undermine your authenticity and uniqueness

What are your thoughts about The Guiding Voice platform?
TGV is a brilliant platform that gives voices to people and their stories. And stories have the power to change people's lives altogether!

One Quote or Anecdote that you strongly believe in?
It's not always a drop in the ocean, but it's always an entire ocean in a drop" by ~Rumi.

> **Question to Self:**
> Q. How can I contribute to breaking barriers and addressing challenges in my own professional sphere?

Tune into Dipika's Episode here:

21

Manav Sony: Inspiring Change for a Better Tomorrow.

A fearless young change maker who strongly believes that "Life is not easy, it's how easy you make it."

When someone talks of Kolkata, the first thing that clicks us is - a city full of chaos, that pulses with life and embraces its rich cultural heritage. And in the bustling streets of Kolkata, where the dynamic blend of cultures and traditions forms a vibrant life fabric, there is a young individual who stands apart. Manav Sony is an aspiring career coach with a deep passion to work on social issues. Manav firmly believes that if people join forces and help one another, they could overcome any challenge and create a beautiful life. He understands that life isn't always easy, it is all about how you make it easier.

Talking of Kolkata, it is where Manav Sony's journey as a young change-maker began. It was during his time in law college that he realized his education held a greater purpose beyond acquiring legal knowledge. It was shaping him into a leader with the power to bring about transformation.

It was in the second year of college that Manav's calling truly took hold. With a fire in his heart and a vision burning bright, he rallied together a team of like-minded individuals. Around 60-70 people, including his juniors and batch mates, joined him on a mission to sensitize the city about the power of mediation—a peaceful and alternative approach to resolving disputes, sparing individuals the daunting path of litigation.

Taking to the streets, Manav and his team conducted live demonstrations, educating people about the benefits of mediation. Their tireless efforts touched lives and sparked a change within the community. Buoyed by their success, Manav and his team set their sights on even greater challenges, seeking to address the pressing issues of children's education and hygiene.

Their collective footsteps led them to the slums, orphanages, and children's organizations of Kolkata. Armed with books, compassion, and an unwavering belief in the transformative power of education, they imparted basic knowledge and English language skills to underprivileged children. Through these initiatives, they sowed seeds of hope and opportunity, nurturing a generation with the tools to break free from the chains of poverty.

Driven by an unyielding love for his city and a deep sense of responsibility, Manav did not stop there. He recognized the urgent need for environmental conservation and preservation. Drawing upon his past experiences running an NGO, which tirelessly worked to clean drains, and ponds, and collaborate with multinational corporations for Corporate Social Responsibility (CSR) initiatives, Manav instilled this profound value in his team. Together, they took up the arduous task of safeguarding Kolkata's fragile ecosystem. Armed with determination and a strong belief in the interconnectedness of humans and the environment, they embarked on projects that aimed to restore and protect natural resources. Their actions spoke louder than words as they toiled tirelessly, clearing debris, raising awareness, and instilling a sense of responsibility within the community.

For Manav, change was not just an abstract concept—it was a beautiful feeling that he believed everyone should strive for. Inspired by Albert Einstein's timeless words, "***The world as we have created it is a process of our thinking. It cannot be changed without changing our thinking,***" Manav became the driving force behind the movement for a better society.

However, Manav's journey as a young change-maker was not without its share of challenges. The path he walked demanded qualities such as leadership, critical thinking, and effective execution. Through his interactions with numerous individuals and communities, he witnessed both the extraordinary resilience of the human spirit and the harsh realities that sought to hinder progress. However, he chose to move ahead, fueled by the relentless support of his committed team and assistance from local authorities.

Amid his journey, Manav experienced a profound encounter that would forever alter his perspective. A fateful interaction with RJ Jimmy Tangree, the beloved host of a popular radio show in Kolkata, bestowed upon him a pearl of wisdom. On a particularly difficult day, Manav reached out to the airwaves, seeking solace and guidance. In response, RJ Jimmy shared a simple yet profound truth:

"Life is not easy, it is actually how easy you make it."

Those words resonated deeply within Manav's soul, imprinting upon him a philosophy that would guide his every step.

Armed with his experiences and hard-won insights, Manav had a wealth of advice to offer those yearning to make a significant impact in their own careers. He urged them to cultivate personal growth from their very first year of college, to strive for excellence, and to stand out among their peers. In the face of obstacles, he encouraged resilience and the relentless pursuit of self-improvement. Above all, he emphasized the power of collaboration among fellow young change-makers—a collective force capable of driving monumental societal change.

And so, Manav Sony's journey as a young change-maker continued. Inspired by his own experiences, he aspired to ignite a flame of hope in the hearts of others, inviting them to join the movement and together create a brighter future for all.

And now here's the time to discover the lighter side of Manav's personality, as he delved into a rapid-fire adventure, sharing anecdotes, dreams, and a glimpse into the playful spirit that made him truly one-of-a-kind.

What is your favourite failure?
When I went for a mediation awareness project and was stopped to do so by local goons in the area.

Can you mention some hardships you went through while going through your life/career journey?
I failed in certain projects because I did not have any particular knowledge or skill which was required to be applied. Also, I started to lose many important people from my team because the workload was becoming high and I did not have the funds to compensate for their efforts

What is your planned vs actual career path?
I had planned to become a Real Estate Lawyer at a reputed law firm but now I am aiming to open a social enterprise on public redressal. Society issues have made me understand a lot of things and I feel I was born to make Kolkata city beautiful and clean.

What is the major turning point in your life?
When I see my parents working so well and have now expanded their business to a larger level. My mother left her school teaching job and thus joined hands with my dad in supporting him throughout.

Who influenced you the most & how?
Mr Jimmy Tangree from 91.9 Friends FM has been a motivator for me. I call him every Friday and share my problem. He has always tried to guide me like a father does to his son and therefore supports my relationship with my girlfriend. He is very eager to see us both married.

What is one incident that transformed your life?
I saw a truck falling at a place which was full of waste and still people did not come forward to help the driver. I had been filing complaints about the land a lot of times but the government failed to listen to me.

What is one thing you would like to do differently in the past?
Work so hard to bring social change in Kolkata and set an example for citizens.

**What's your Vision/Goal/ in life and what are you
trying to achieve?**
I want to run my social enterprise where I can
understand the issues of common people and thus help
them to get them solved easily.

**What's the craziest/Naughtiest thing you have done
in childhood?**
My brother and I have broken a lot of windows and tube
lights while playing cricket at our colony and even made
prank calls to our friends by changing voices and phone
numbers. We have even landed into trouble for doing
this but we enjoyed doing it together.

**What is one Hidden/unknown/least known fact
about you?**
I am not a shy and introverted person which I show to
people. In reality, I love to talk a lot and make good
friendships with meaningful people.

**What is your favourite fantasy gadget that you want
for yourself/want to invent?**
A superpower where I get the strength and power to
fight the goons in the city who are against local
development and therefore a power of persuasion
which can help me make people understand the
problems and make them act in a civilized way as
instructed.

If you are not at work, what do you like doing?
I call up my friends and chat with them for hours. Apart
from that, I look after my health by jogging and playing
sports like cricket or table tennis.

How do you keep yourself up-to-date? Please share links or references to websites/blogs/books etc.
The Alchemist by Paulo Coelho, *Monk Who Sold His Ferrari* by Robin Sharma and some slow music

What is one piece of advice you want to give to the youngsters in the field?
There will be times when you will face challenges. Never get afraid of that and keep moving forward. Have the best people around you who can support you whenever you need them. Also, develop good leadership skills.

What are your thoughts about The Guiding Voice platform?
The Guiding Voice is doing an excellent job by bringing up stories on their platform which have been unheard, and those people are not noticed by the media or even by their neighbours. I am happy to see the team doing so well and bringing up unheard voices forward.

One Quote or Anecdote that you strongly believe in?
"Life is never easy, it's how easy you make it"

Question to Self:
Am I challenging my potential enough to make an impact on the world around me?

Tune into Manav's Episode here:

22

Anveshi Gutta: A Journey to Sustainability.

Personal convictions, urban development experiences, and the birth of Atquest Sustainable Solutions; Anveshi's journey is about embracing changes and shaping the Future.

"Sustainability": We are sure you must have listened to this word a zillion times by now! It is not only reflected in the choices individuals make in day-to-day life but also in responsible living and forward-thinking initiatives. And individuals like Anveshi Gutta stand at the forefront of a movement towards a sustainable future. He is not only practising sustainable living but also exploring the realms of eco-conscious living. Expanding it to professional endeavours to harmonize with the rhythms of positive change. Anveshi, the CEO of Atquest Sustainable Solutions Private Limited, epitomizes the spirit of this chapter—a narrative that transcends mere career trajectories and delves into the profound commitment to a world where sustainability is not just a buzzword but a way of life. From his early days in IT consulting to navigating the complexities of social impact, Anveshi's journey is an example of the transformative power of sustainable practices. He started his career journey as an IT consultant. He was leading the smart cities consulting engagement for cities predominantly in developing markets within India, UAE, Qatar and South Africa. It is in this role that he was invited at various conferences and universities to be a keynote speaker on topics related to urban development. He became a member of Technology and Standardization Initiatives at the *Bureau of Indian Standards and the Open Group*, where he has advocated the use of technology adaption that drives impact on the key stakeholders, that is, the citizens themselves.

With his exposure to sustainability and environmental challenges across the world, he became conscious about creating a social impact and making people aware at a wider scale. In 2002, Anveshi left his job and stepped into Entrepreneurship with his venture Atquest Sustainable Solutions Private Limited- *a social enterprise that focuses on urban sustainable living.* **Anveshi's commitment to learning, unlearning, and relearning since 2002 served as a guiding principle in his life.**

His unyielding openness to new ideas and perspectives becomes a foundation for his success in both personal and professional realms.

The Shift to Sustainability
An IT consultant turned into an Entrepreneur for Sustainability awareness!

Why sustainability?
Anveshi challenges this question and proposes, "Why not?"
His decision to embark on a career in sustainability is not only a professional choice but a personal commitment. He explored and adapted a green lifestyle—an intimate journey shared with his wife. What worked for them became the seed of an idea: could it work for others too?

The discussion extended beyond the boardrooms of his office into the heart of corporate decision-making. Transitioning into sustainability wasn't a seamless endeavour. Anveshi reflects on the mixed bag of experiences, the challenges, and the revelations that characterized this shift.

But since it worked for him at a personal level, he took it
further. In his journey to learn, he explored the
emerging landscape of sustainability as a concept,
shedding light on ESG (Environmental, Social and
Governance factors to assess the sustainability of
companies and countries) considerations in corporate
decision-making. He dived deep into the varied
opportunities in this dynamic field, understanding its
impact on diverse sectors and the skills required for
aspiring professionals. His belief that all businesses are
driven by the intent and motivation behind made his
organization a success.

For aspiring professionals, Anveshi underscores the
alignment of sustainability courses with industry needs.
He encourages mastery of standards like GRI, SASB,
CDP, and CDSB, equipping individuals to stay
competitive in this ever-evolving sector.
He explored and conveyed the message to a wider
audience in terms of a shift from traditional capitalism to
stakeholder capitalism and the global commitment to
achieving net-zero emissions.

Amid these discussions, we had Anveshi raising a
poignant question—*how can humanity remain blind
to the imminent danger that our choices pose to the
planet?*

He ponders how we, as a species, can remain
seemingly oblivious to the impending peril that looms
on the horizon. It's disheartening to acknowledge our
shared selfishness, as we engage in actions that we
know are detrimental not only to our present but to the
well-being of future generations. We are consciously

making choices that could lead our offspring, and generations beyond, into a bleak future.

This dilemma has left him bewildered, and he admits that he's yet to find a satisfactory answer to why individuals, including himself, sometimes adopt such a perspective on life.

Companies have historically prioritized revenue over sustainability, particularly evident in the electronics industry, with products like mobile phones and computers. It's disheartening to discover that certain components, like RAM slots in computers, are sealed to prevent user upgrades, pushing consumers towards buying entirely new devices. This approach raises concerns about the environmental impact, specifically the carbon footprint associated with electronic waste.

There's a compelling argument for adopting a different approach, similar to what Tesla is doing with their cars. They allow customers to upgrade their existing vehicles to the next version rather than compelling them to purchase entirely new ones. This concept of expandable and upgradeable mobile phones aligns with the sustainability goals advocated here. It emphasizes the need for the tech industry to not only focus on revenue but also consider the long-term environmental consequences of their products.

Anveshi's answer to this is—Circularity. It involves designing products and materials in a way that minimizes their disposal in landfills. The concept revolves around whether something is 'designed for the dump' or 'designed for life.' In the past, products like

TVs and refrigerators were built to last for many years, but the current trend is to create products with shorter lifespans, leading to a significant increase in electronic waste or e-waste.

Anveshi's message for younger entrepreneurs is a call to action: start your journey early, prioritize responsible consumption, and, above all, stay open to learning.

Anveshi raised the right questions, at the right time! His journey is driven by passion, responsibility, and an unwavering commitment to learning in the pursuit of a sustainable future.

And while we leave you with food for thought on how to live sustainably and make conscious purchase choices, here is a rapid-fire round we had with Anveshi. A further glimpse into exploring the life of this change-maker!

What is your favourite failure?
Considering how much I love what I do today, I would say the inability to answer my true calling early in my professional life is my biggest setback.

What are the hardships you went through while going through your life/career journey?
I've been fortunate not to have gone through tough times. I say this with conviction because I have seen the hardships that my parents went through as they brought us up. In comparison, I've had a relatively smooth ride. There were little bumps along the way when I've had sleepless nights to address some pressing issues. These were mostly because of the

career shifts I've been through in the last couple of decades. I shifted my career path at least 4 times and each time, I've had to go through tough rounds of learn-perform-prove. But I guess, that kept me engrossed and interested too.

What was your planned vs actual career path?
My career path has been a story of multiple shifts. As I look back, I don't think I started with a well-crafted and planned career path. Over the years, as I did my MBA I believe the entrepreneurship bug bit me. Then, as I did business process consulting and smart cities consulting, I believe I graduated into a professional who led by example. Today, I have brought those together as I lead At Quest Sustainable Solutions.

What is the turning point in your life?
For a small-town boy, the turning point must be when I decided to pursue my engineering in Bangalore and come out of my safe shell.

One person that influenced you the most & how?
Mr. Sridhar Vembu and Mr. Narayana Murthy - both for the humility they display despite being so well-accomplished.

One incident that transformed your life?
When I started engineering, I wasn't able to clearly distinguish between right-click and left-click on the mouse, and my friends were already learning OOPS concepts. That shook me and got me thinking. I had to put in extra effort to learn extensively and catch up. To date, the hunger for learning refuses to come down.

One thing you would do differently in the past?
I would have turned entrepreneur at least 10-15 years
back.

Your Vision/Goal/ in life and what are you trying to achieve?
The only outcome that I constantly aim for is to ensure
that the people around me see value in what I bring to
the table. I have always been hungry for the results,
more than the money. I have always been hungry for
acknowledgement of true impact. Today, the goal I
pursue is to make sure that our work inspires people
and impacts the planet positively.

A hidden/unknown/least known fact about you
In order of priority, I have a fetish for spectacles,
cufflinks and fountain pens.

Favourite fantasy gadget that you want for yourself/want to invent?
A universal magic wand that drives behavioural change,
in every citizen on this planet

If you are not at work, what do you like doing?
Spending time with friends or family over a sport, over a
meal, over just chitter-chatter. Just be amongst people.

How do you keep yourself up to date?
To be up to date with regard to my field of work - I
subscribe to relevant newsletters, listen to webinars
and podcasts, read reports and technical papers, and
network extensively on LinkedIn to stay up-to-date on
current affairs - I read the good-old newspaper diligently

every day, apart from news apps that keep me posted with relevant notifications.

What are your thoughts about The Guiding Voice platform?
Shaping careers is one of the toughest tasks and TGV has taken the bull by its horns. The perseverance and passion with which the platform is run always meant that the positive impact was bound to happen.

One quote or Anecdote that you strongly believe in.
There are far, far better things ahead than any we leave behind.

> ***Question to Self:***
> Q. How can I contribute to sustainable living in my own life and community, and what steps can I take to create positive change for a more sustainable future?

Tune into Anveshi's Episode here:

ABOUT TGV

The Global Odyssey: TGV Emerges as the World's Only Tri-lingual Podcast Listed in the Global Top 3%

In the vast universe of digital content, **The Guiding Voice** (TGV) has emerged as a beacon of guidance, a platform dedicated to shaping the destinies of students, professionals at all levels, leaders and entrepreneurs worldwide. This section unravels the compelling journey of TGV, a venture that has not only carved its niche in the podcasting realm but has set a bold vision to impact a minimum of 1 million individuals across the globe in the next two years.

Setting the Stage

On the momentous day of May 17th, 2020, TGV took its inaugural steps into the digital landscape. At the time of writing, it is positioned in the Global Top 3%, which stands as a testament to the dedication and vision of its founder, Naveen Samala. The platform is not merely a repository of information; it is a dynamic force, a catalyst for personal and professional development.

The Content Canvas

TGV's content strategy is a diverse mosaic, interwoven with threads of soft skills, behavioural insights, entrepreneurial endeavours and technological wisdom.

The Guiding Voice (English)

Transformation Tuesdays: Launch of personal/self development related episodes
Tech Thursdays: Leadership, entrepreneurship and Technology related episodes.

TGV Telugu
Episodes focusing on career and/or life transformation every Wednesday in Telugu.

TGV Hindi
Episodes focusing on career and/or life transformation every Friday in Hindi.

Naveen Samala firmly believes in spreading the knowledge of bold topics like body shaming, sex education, awareness on periods, LGBTQ, dealing with porn addiction to name a few.

He has covered a range of topics in the realm of life and career supporting Women Empowerment through **TGV Corporate Diva** series, Girl child education empowerment through **TGV Slice of Hope** series.

His next focus is to host the **Global Speaker festival** in Jan 2024. Where 31 episodes will be launched featuring 31 guests from 31 different countries. An initiative like no other ever before.

Numbers at a glance
The platform has released an impressive 404 episodes as of December 6th, 2023 under The Guiding Voice English, 79 episodes in TGV Telugu and 45 episodes in TGV Hindi.

Global Reach
TGV extends its reach across major social media platforms – LinkedIn, Twitter, Facebook, Instagram, and Pinterest. The cumulative viewership, a staggering 30,000+ listeners across 130+ countries, attests to the

global impact of the platform. The engagement on various directories and the YouTube version has become a community-driven movement.

Multilingual Expansion
In the spirit of inclusivity, TGV expanded its linguistic footprint. In 2022, TGV launched its Telugu edition (TGV Telugu). 2023 witnessed the addition of TGV Hindi, introduced on January 27th.

The multilingual approach reflects TGV's commitment to reaching diverse audiences and fostering a global dialogue. And most importantly, preserving the rich cultural heritage in the form of Indian languages. Naveen Samala's vision is to launch in at least 5 to 6 major Indian languages in the next 1 to 3 years.

True dreams will never let you sleep, dream big and chase!!

Acknowledgements

This book is more than just words on paper; it is a collaborative effort, a symphony of support, patience, and encouragement. To those whose unwavering belief fuelled the journey of **TGV Inspiring Lives Volume 2**, we extend our deepest gratitude.

To Family:
You are the pillars of our strength and the roots from which we draw sustenance. Your patience, understanding, and unyielding support have been the bedrock of this endeavour. Thank you for standing by us through the highs and lows.

To Friends:
In laughter and in silence, in celebration and in solace, you've been our constant companions. Your friendship has been a beacon, illuminating the path when the way seemed uncertain. Thank you for being the anchors in our lives.

To TGV Speakers:
You are the heartbeat of this book. Your stories, insights, and experiences have woven a tapestry of inspiration. Each conversation has been a journey, and we are grateful for the privilege of sharing your voices with the world. Thank you for entrusting us with your narratives.

To the TGV Core Team, Audience and Community:
Your enthusiasm and engagement have been the wind beneath our wings. The TGV community is a testament

to the power of connection and shared wisdom. Thank you for being a vital part of this incredible journey.

To Well-Wishers:
Your encouragement, constructive feedback, and positive energy have been invaluable. In your belief, we found renewed motivation. Thank you for being the cheerleaders on this path.

To the Universe:
For orchestrating serendipities, opening doors, and guiding us through the creative process, we express our heartfelt thanks. The universe conspired to make this book a reality, and we are humbled by its cosmic dance.

Special thanks to our friends Sucharitha Karri, Upnit Singh & Basha Mehaboob for proof reading the manuscript and providing their valuable feedback and inputs.

Thanks to Sameer Bhatt and Raaga Pranavi Samala for providing their valuable inputs on the book cover design.

To all those mentioned and the countless others who contributed to this project, directly or indirectly, thank you for being a part of this exciting journey. This book is a collective triumph, and your fingerprints are etched on every page.

INTERACT WITH US

Connect with the **authors** on LinkedIn:

Naveen Samala:
https://www.linkedin.com/in/naveensamala/

Parul Gupta:
https://www.linkedin.com/in/parul-gupta-b4262124/

Connect with the featured **speakers** on LinkedIn or Facebook:

Cathy Nesbitt

https://www.linkedin.com/in/cathynesbitt/

Preeta Pradhan

https://www.linkedin.com/in/emotionalwellnesscoachpre etapradhan/

Joshua Shea

https://www.linkedin.com/in/joshua-shea-7b9932194/

Avrum Weiss

https://www.linkedin.com/in/avrumweissphd/

Mary Alice Arthur

https://www.linkedin.com/in/mary-alice-arthur/

Vidyadhar Prabhudesai

https://www.linkedin.com/in/vidyadhar/

Rob Grover

https://www.linkedin.com/in/rob-grover-msc-a9247415/

Gary Logan

https://www.linkedin.com/in/logangary/

Chitra Singh

https://www.linkedin.com/in/chitra-singh-sampathkumar-sales-mentor/

E. Prabhakar Reddy

https://www.facebook.com/profile.php?id=100009403392646

Alex Benett

https://www.facebook.com/LiteraryBooze

Ramesh Manickavel(Rammy)

https://www.linkedin.com/in/rameshmanickavel/

Suman De

https://www.linkedin.com/in/suman-de-54351a22/

Vinoda Reddy

https://www.facebook.com/spoorthy.reddy.9803

Tribikram Rath

https://www.linkedin.com/in/tri-rath/

Hemalatha Rao

https://www.facebook.com/profile.php?id=1373475110

Yashwant Sai Palaghat

https://www.linkedin.com/in/yaswanthpalaghat/

Omita Gaikwad

https://www.linkedin.com/in/omitagaikwad/

Sourish Ghosh

https://www.linkedin.com/in/sourishghosh/

Vijay K Banda

https://www.linkedin.com/in/vijaybanda/

Deepika Trehan

https://www.linkedin.com/in/dipika-trehan/

Manav Soni

https://www.linkedin.com/in/manav-sony-6a630a19a/

Anveshi Gutta

https://www.linkedin.com/in/anveshigutta/

Check out our **TGV Inspiring Lives Volume 1**

Kindle Edition:

https://www.amazon.in/dp/B0BQ3VZHH9?ref_=cm_sw_r_cp_ud_dp_6K6W41H3DCJFPM4RW0A5

Paperback (Available in India at the time of this publication):

https://www.amazon.in/Inspiring-Lives-Naseha-Sameen/dp/B0BQ2TPDR3/ref=tmm_pap_swatch_0?_encoding=UTF8&qid=&sr=

Visit Our Website

https://www.theguidingvoice.net

https://www.naveensamala.com

Subscribe to **Think Hatke with TGV** Newsletter on LinkedIn: https://www.linkedin.com/build-relation/newsletter-follow?entityUrn=6897044335829884928

Subscribe to our blogs on **Medium**:

TGV Podcasts

English

YouTube:
http://youtube.com/@theguidingvoice

Apple podcast:
https://podcasts.apple.com/in/podcast/the-guiding-voice/id1511786719

Spotify:
https://open.spotify.com/show/1GvX6tvmfelawEba0F6KS4

Hindi

YouTube:

https://www.youtube.com/@tgvhindi

Apple podcast:

https://podcasts.apple.com/in/podcast/tgv-hindi/id1668148953

Spotify:

https://open.spotify.com/show/2wyLNGG0tsHucmhRauh4o3?si=1615099d371f4793

Telugu

YouTube:
https://www.youtube.com/@tgvtelugu

Apple podcast:
https://podcasts.apple.com/in/podcast/tgv-telugu/id1643541921

Spotify:
https://open.spotify.com/show/3fCfHwoFIiehHJSPcgoX4I?si=44f0d20403a147e1